The Light We Birth:

Conscious Parenting, Star Children, and the New Earth Rising

by

Anastasia Spencer

Copyright

© 2025 Anastasia Spencer. All rights reserved.

No portion of this book may be reproduced or transmitted in any form or by any means without the written permission of the author.

www.portalofrebirth.com

Dedication

To my son—whose light, laughter, and love inspire my every heartbeat. You are the reason this book was born.

I cherish every moment spent with you—playing, laughing, learning, and exploring the wonders of life together. I am deeply grateful for this life and for you, my dear son, who has been one of my greatest teachers. Through you, I have learned about higher consciousness, unconditional love, pure joy, and the sacred wisdom of Star Children. You are my light and my gentle reminder of how to return to wholeness.

And to all children of the world—may you always remember the brilliance of your soul and the sacred love that brought you here.

Dear parents,

I invite you to connect deeply with the sacred journey of conscious pre-conception, pregnancy, birth, and parenting. When we approach these stages with awareness and intention, we create a nurturing space where Star Children—souls who come to share their unique gifts—can feel loved, seen, and supported. These extraordinary children are here to help elevate humanity, and it is our purpose as parents and guides to offer them the compassion, respect, and understanding they need to flourish.

This book is for mothers and fathers who wish to recognize the profound influence that pregnancy and the first three years of life have on a child's future. These early stages form not only the foundation of physical development but also shape emotional, psychological, and spiritual growth. By understanding this, parents can better support their children in becoming balanced, conscious individuals. Awareness of developmental milestones allows parents to create environments that foster curiosity, confidence, and self-expression. When parents are attuned to their child's emotional and spiritual needs, they naturally provide the guidance and encouragement essential for healthy growth on every level.

Both parents play vital roles in this sacred process from pre-conception through mindful parenting and personal healing. When mothers and fathers engage equally, children feel safe, valued, and supported. However, to guide a child consciously, parents must first heal themselves. Addressing unresolved pain, stress, and trauma helps release generational patterns and creates a harmonious family dynamic built on love rather than fear. Although fathers may not experience pregnancy physically, their energetic connection to the process is profound. From the moment conception is known, fathers often feel a powerful wave of emotions—joy, excitement, anxiety, and even fear. Each heartbeat they hear and each kick they feel deepens their bond with the baby and transforms their identity. Their journey mirrors that of the mother in emotional intensity, though expressed differently. This book honors that sacred connection and explores the father's essential role in creating an environment of love and security for both mother and child.

Becoming a mother has been one of the most transformative experiences of my life. It has taught me patience, unconditional love, and resilience. Nurturing another soul has opened my heart and expanded my capacity for compassion. This sacred role became a catalyst for profound personal growth and spiritual awakening. My own healing journey began with a desire to understand myself more deeply and to release the trauma of my past. Years of study and practice in hypnotherapy, trauma healing, and intuitive development led me to my true calling—helping parents transform the emotional wounds and limiting beliefs that unconsciously shape their families. Through this work, I have witnessed the extraordinary transformation that unfolds when parents heal. They not only free themselves from pain but also prevent those wounds from being passed on to their children.

Supporting families in this way fills me with purpose and joy, inspiring me to help Star Children recognize their inner light and navigate this world with confidence and grace. I relate deeply to these children because, from a young age, I too felt different and out of place in the ordinary world. I was highly sensitive, intuitive, and attuned to something beyond the physical realm. Unfortunately, I had no one with whom I could share what I was experiencing. This is why I was guided to create this book, so parents can become the steady anchors, loving support, and safe place their Star Children can turn to. This calling also inspired me to create an online course, "Sacred Pregnancy and Conscious Parenting." My mission is to share various tools and practices that help parents consciously prepare for conception, nurture their babies with awareness, and raise children in alignment with love and higher wisdom. This vision also led me to found Our Dream Academy for Gifted Children, a place where each child's unique talents and spirit are honored. Our goal is to empower children to flourish and to live in alignment with their soul's purpose.

Drawing upon my professional experience and personal journey as a mother, educator, and conscious guide, I have designed this book to be both practical and heart-centered. It combines years of research, thousands of healing sessions, and real experience to support parents on their sacred path. I also encourage you to explore *The Sacred Birthing and Pregnancy Journey Workbook*, available on Amazon and at www.portalofrebirth.com/books. This companion resource offers guided exercises and healing tools to help mothers connect with their babies, bodies, and inner strength.

To all readers who walk this path with me—thank you. Your dedication to conscious living and loving parenting is what will reshape the world.

I am profoundly grateful to live my purpose each day while raising my son and watching him grow into his highest potential. It is my deepest joy to see him thrive—rooted in love, guided by wisdom, and connected to the beauty of Earth.

May this book serve as a light on your journey!

A Blessing for the Conscious Parent

Walk this path with grace and courage—
even when the way feels challenging,
even when your heart is tender and raw.

Remember that the light you nurture in your child
is the same divine flame that burns within you—
eternal, wise, and unbreakable.

See your child not as something to mold,
but as a soul to honor—a mirror of the infinite
reflecting back who you truly are.

Let your home become a sanctuary of gentleness—
a place where sensitivity is sacred strength,
intuition is trusted more than fear,
and laughter, silence, and tears
each hold their rightful place.

Have patience to listen beyond words,
hear the quiet language of your child's heart,
and to trust that every moment—
even the messy, uncertain ones—is filled with grace.

Allow every challenge to open your heart wider,
revealing the hidden gold within each trial.
Know that healing is not perfection—
it is presence, the courage to love through it all.

Feel yourself guided by glowing light,
supported by ancestors,

who dreamed this awakening into being,
and surrounded by angels
who whisper to you: You are not alone.

Let your journey as a conscious parent
awaken the deeper truth—
that love, in its purest form,
is both the teacher and the lesson,
the beginning and the return,
the very heartbeat of creation itself.

— **Anastasia Spencer**

Table of Contents

Dedication 5

A Blessing for the Conscious Parent 9

PART I: The Light We Birth

Chapter 1: The Call to Conscious Parenting: Awakening the Light Within 15

Chapter 2: The New Children, Star Children, and the Shifting Earth 19

Chapter 3: Signs and Traits of Star Children 29

Chapter 4: Parents' Inner Healing to Help Star Children Thrive 35

Chapter 5: The Star Child as a Mirror 43

Chapter 6: Preparing the Vessel 49

Chapter 7: The Journey of Conscious Pregnancy and Birth 53

Chapter 8: The Heart of Conscious Parenting 65

Chapter 9: The Sacred Journey of Parenting 73

Chapter 10: Creating Sacred Space: The Importance of the Home Environment .. 85

Chapter 11: The Sacred Role of the Father 89

Chapter 12: The Sacred Role of the Mother 94

Chapter 13: Guiding and Nurturing Star Children 99

Chapter 14: The New Earth Family: Co-creating a Conscious Future 111

Conclusion 118

PART II: Inner Toolkit for Conscious Parents

The Practice of Self-Care and Self-Reflection 122

A Guided Meditation for Conscious Parents 142

Gratitude and Light 144

A Blessing for You and Your Child 145

Acknowledgments 147

About Author 148

PART I

The Light We Birth

Chapter 1

The Call to Conscious Parenting: Awakening the Light Within

There comes a moment in every soul's journey when life places a sacred responsibility in our hands—the guidance of another soul. This moment, whether expected or mysterious, marks the unfolding of a deeper spiritual contract: the agreement to become a conscious parent.

To parent consciously is to remember that our children are not ours to shape, but ours to witness. They come not as blank slates waiting to be written upon, but as radiant beings, already whole, already wise, and carrying ancient codes of remembrance within their hearts. Some of them are intuitive and deeply sensitive—the ones who feel the unseen currents of emotion and energy, arriving to awaken not only their own light but also ours.

They are mirrors of what the world has forgotten: tenderness, truth, empathy, and the quiet knowing that everything is connected. To walk beside them is to enter a deep spiritual journey that softens the ego, expands compassion, and reveals the true meaning of presence.

The Sacred Invitation and Soul Contract Between Parent and Child

Parenting an intuitive, highly sensitive child, or Star Child, is not an ordinary task; it is a sacred initiation. These children arrive carrying frequencies of awareness that can feel both wondrous and bewildering. They sense the emotions of others before they have words to name their own. They may be unsettled by noise, conflict, or the dissonance between words and truth. Their sensitivity is not fragility, but it is attunement. Through them, humanity remembers how to feel again. But to nurture their gifts, we must first awaken our own. Conscious parenting begins not with the child, but with the parent's willingness to heal—to return to stillness, listen, and embody the love they wish their child to know.

Before birth, souls gather in luminous councils beyond time, sharing their intentions for the journey ahead. Some choose to return together, one as the guide and one as the mirror, to fulfill shared lessons of love, trust, and growth. These sacred agreements are not random; they are orchestrated with divine precision. Each soul chooses the perfect family, timing, and circumstances to awaken deeper wisdom and compassion within all involved.

Star Children often choose parents who are ready or nearly ready to awaken to higher consciousness. Their arrival is never accidental. They come to catalyze transformation, illuminate what has been forgotten, and help heal ancestral patterns through love. You may have felt their presence long before conception, perhaps as a whisper in your dreams or a subtle stirring in your heart. When such a soul comes into your life, it is a sign that your own evolution is unfolding.

Even in moments of exhaustion or uncertainty, your connection is a sacred design. Your child's sensitivity may awaken parts of you that have been buried for years, including grief you did not realize you carried, tenderness you learned to conceal, and dreams you thought had faded away. Through this, the child calls you home to yourself. Their light touches every shadow, not to judge, but to bring healing and remembrance. Each emotion they mirror is an invitation: Can you love this, too? Can you hold this, without judgment, without trying to fix it? Can you remember that your presence is what they need most?

Parent and child walk hand in hand, weaving light through generations. Your soul agreed to this meeting long before your first breath together.

You are both teachers and students in the same sacred classroom of life. As you guide your child, they quietly guide you as well, awakening patience, expanding empathy, and revealing a love that transforms all it touches. In honoring this soul contract, you awaken to the profound truth that parenting is not merely a responsibility, but a spiritual path. Every challenge becomes an opportunity to grow in awareness, and every moment of connection becomes an act of divine remembrance. Through this sacred dance of souls, love expands, healing ripples through your lineage, and new light enters the world.

The Awakening of the Parent

The journey of conscious parenting dismantles illusion. It invites us to move beyond inherited patterns, the familiar habits of fear, control, and performance, and to begin cultivating awareness instead. We are asked to listen more deeply, speak more truthfully, and love more freely. The sensitive child cannot thrive in pretense; they feel every vibration of authenticity or its absence. They call forth integrity not as moral perfection, but as energetic alignment.

This awakening is rarely gentle at first. The child's sensitivity may mirror your own unhealed wounds. Their tears may echo your childhood pain. Their silence may reflect your forgotten longing for peace. But through this, you are reborn. Conscious parenting is not about shaping your child into light; it is about remembering that you are light, too.

Conscious parenting begins with seeing our children as whole and aware from the start. Their sensitivity and intuition invite us to slow down, heal old patterns, and show up with honesty and presence. Parenting a Star Child is a sacred partnership. They reflect what needs care within us and guide us toward greater clarity and compassion. Through this connection, we learn that parenting is not about perfection, but about growing alongside our child. Each moment of awareness strengthens the bond, supports healing, and helps both parent and child step into a more grounded, loving way of being.

Chapter 2

The New Children, Star Children, and the Shifting Earth

We are living in a time of great energetic transformation. The Earth herself is awakening, recalibrating into the vibration of love, compassion, and interconnection. The children arriving now are attuned to this new frequency. They are the bridge between the old world and the one being born. These children sense unity. They feel the pain of disconnection in families, in societies, and in the planet itself, as if it were their own. These souls choose to incarnate on Earth not out of obligation, but out of love. Each arrival is a spark sent to illuminate humanity's evolution and to remind us of unity, peace, and the infinite creative potential within us all. They are an embodiment of joy. Those children hold no karmic debt and radiate unconditional love. Fearless, compassionate, and imaginative, they are here to shape a new world where love becomes the guiding force and creativity becomes the way forward.

The Whisper of the Stars

Long before the first words were written, humanity looked up at the night sky and wondered who we are, where we came from, and why we are here. Across deserts and oceans, under pyramids and within ancient temples, people once spoke of the stars as living beings, as guardians who guided them, teachers who inspired them, and ancestors who watched over them. They told stories of light descending to Earth, of souls who carried the memory of other worlds. Those stories were not simply myths; they were memory.

Every soul on Earth has cosmic roots, but some souls known as Star Children carry those roots closer to the surface. They come into this world with eyes that seem to hold galaxies, hearts that feel too deeply for their age, and a quiet remembrance that this planet, beautiful as it is, is not their first home. They are here to help it remember its light.

If you are reading this and something inside you stirs like a faint memory, a pulse of recognition then you may be feeling the echo of your own star origin. That gentle vibration in your heart is the language of remembrance, calling you back to truth. Many adults who are now awakening were once the Star Children of earlier decades, sensitive souls who carried light in a world that was not yet ready to receive it. They learned to hide their brilliance to survive, yet the light within them never dimmed. Now, it rises once more. The time has come for us all to look up and remember that we belong to something vast, ancient, and beautiful. The stars are not far away; they live within us. Every heartbeat echoes the rhythm of the cosmos. Every breath is a thread connecting heaven and Earth. Star Children who arrive now come to remind humanity of this sacred truth that we are not separate, and we never were. Their eyes often hold a wisdom beyond years, for they remember the unity that lies beyond duality. They call us to remember our own origins, our divine essence, and our purpose in this grand unfolding.

If you are a Star Child reading these words, know this: Your mission is already unfolding, even when you cannot yet see the full picture. You are not behind, and you are not alone. Every challenge, every moment of sensitivity, every wave of emotion is part of your awakening. You are here because Earth called, and you answered. You are here because the Divine Spirit needed a voice, and it chose yours. You are here to bridge worlds, bring the wisdom of the stars into the heartbeat of humanity, ground heaven into soil, and weave light into the fabric of everyday life. You are both cosmic and human, infinite and tender, radiant and real. Shine, beloved soul. The world is ready for your light. Your very existence is a message of hope, a sign that the universe is unfolding and awakening through you. The time of forgetting is over. The time of remembrance has begun.

The Collective Awakening

Humanity's awakening is not sudden; it unfolds in waves. Each generation of souls arrives with a distinct purpose, carrying codes of light that activate new levels of awareness within the collective. Like the tides, these waves build upon one another, rising and receding, preparing the way for the next.

The first waves of Star Children, referred to as the Indigos, incarnated to disrupt outdated patterns and prepare the way for what would come. They are the system challengers, the truth-tellers, and the catalysts for change. Their spirits carry the frequency of courage and discernment. They question authority, resist limitation, and expose what no longer serves. Many of them faced misunderstanding or resistance because they were born into a world not yet ready to see through their eyes. Yet their purpose was clear: to shatter the walls of complacency and ignite the spark of freedom in human consciousness.

Then came the Crystal Children, gentle yet powerful souls whose purpose was to heal what the Indigos had uncovered. Their energy radiates harmony, empathy, and forgiveness. They remind humanity of the importance of love and emotional truth. Their presence soothes conflict and invites unity, often through creativity, art, or silent understanding.

Following them is the Rainbow Children, who are vibrant, expressive, and filled with joy. They bring color where there was gray, laughter where there was fear, and possibility where there was despair. They embody unconditional love, teaching us that spirituality is not solemn, but alive, playful, and woven through every experience of being human.

Now a new generation is emerging, children born after 2020 who are known by many as the Golden Children. These radiant souls carry the synthesis of all previous waves. They embody balance between action and peace, intellect and intuition, and transcendence. Within them lives both the warrior's courage and the healer's compassion. They are born with crystalline clarity of purpose, able to navigate the digital and spiritual realms with equal grace. Their presence signals a great turning point in human evolution. It is the era when love and awareness begin to shape society more than power or fear.

Together, these generations form a luminous bridge across time, weaving a planetary transformation that will not be led by governments or corporations but by hearts. They are the architects of a new Earth, guided not by hierarchy but by harmony. Through them, humanity learns to live not in separation but in co-creation with all of life. And as each wave of Star Children rises, so too does our collective remembrance; we are one family of light, journeying together through the infinite unfolding of the cosmos.

Who Are Star Children?

Star Children are highly intuitive, sensitive, and gifted souls born with a deep sense of purpose. They come into this world carrying the memory of higher realms, a knowing that love is the true nature of existence. Their mission is to help elevate collective consciousness and guide humanity toward harmony and unity. Even as infants, they hold an ancient presence, with eyes that seem lit by starlight and hearts that respond instinctively to truth, energy, and emotion rather than to words. These children are profoundly empathetic and energetically attuned. They can sense subtle emotional or environmental shifts that others may overlook like the tension in a room, the sadness behind a smile, the unspoken stories in another's heart. For them, the world can sometimes feel too loud, too fast, or too heavy. Loud environments, harsh words, or unresolved conflict can easily unsettle their delicate nervous systems. They may need extra time in stillness, moments in nature, quiet reflection, or gentle reassurance to recalibrate their energy.

Star Children often carry within them an awareness of the unseen. They may speak of memories from before birth, describe energies or colors around people, or express wisdom beyond their years. Their creativity flows naturally through art, music, dreams, and empathy. When they are seen and encouraged, they become channels of healing and inspiration, offering insights that touch the hearts of those around them. If there is no understanding and mindful guidance, their sensitivity can become overwhelming. Also, they might struggle to find their balance because of the fast-paced world driven by noise, screens, and disconnection. Overstimulation may lead them to withdraw, daydream, or retreat into solitude. At other times, they may release frustration, rebellion, or powerful emotion, not as an act of defiance but as a call for deeper connection and energetic safety. It is essential to remember that these behaviors are not flaws but signals. A Star Child's sensitivity is not a weakness; it is a sacred instrument finely tuned to the vibrations of truth and love. What they need most is not correction but attunement, offered by parents, teachers, and caregivers who can meet them with presence, patience, and genuine openness.

Every Star Child thrives in an environment that honors their authenticity and rhythm. When parents slow down and truly see their child beyond expectations or norms, they create a sanctuary where the child's spirit can unfold naturally. In such spaces, confidence blossoms, intuition deepens, and empathy becomes a strength rather than a burden.

These children are here to help humanity remember its wholeness. Through their presence, they awaken others to love, truth, and self-discovery. When supported with understanding, they become luminous beacons, bridges between worlds, teachers of peace, and architects of a new Earth. The more we listen to them, the more we rediscover the forgotten language of the soul.

A Bridge Between Worlds

Humanity stands at a turning point. As technology accelerates and global consciousness expands, the world experiences both awakening and turmoil. The Star Children are the bridge between these two realities. They feel the pain of the planet as if it were their own body, and yet they also hold the blueprint for its healing. They are the gardeners of a new consciousness. Their tools are empathy, creativity, and love. Their mission is not to convert or preach; it is simply to be and live as reminders of what humanity can become.

To understand Star Children is to expand our view of life itself. They are not "better" or "higher" than anyone else; they belong to the same human family, carrying a frequency aligned with compassion and expanded awareness. Whether seen as gifted empaths or highly sensitive souls, their existence invites us all to awaken. They remind us that we too are made of stardust, that every human is both cosmic and earthly, infinite and finite, divine and human.

Star Children are not coming to change the world for us. They are here to awaken the change within us.

The Wisdom They Carry

Star Children often speak truths beyond their years. They may express profound insights about life, death, nature, or compassion in simple, poetic ways. They are the philosophers of the new era, blending innocence with ancient remembrance. Their wisdom flows from their connection to Source, a living current of consciousness that has not been dimmed by conditioning. Many of these children have vivid dreams, imaginary friends who are not so imaginary, or a deep concern for animals and the Earth.

Their connection to the unseen is not fantasy; it is remembrance. Our task as parents is not to close these portals but to help them integrate their sensitivity safely into the physical world. We guide them in grounding and teaching them that it is possible to be fully human and fully luminous at once.

The Starseed Mission

At the heart of every Star Child lies a simple truth: they came to Earth to help humanity remember love. Some fulfill this mission through quiet kindness, some through art or innovation, and others through the way they simply radiate peace in their everyday lives. Their task is not grand in the worldly sense, but it is energetic, invisible, and deeply sacred.

They anchor light as well as they hold compassion in places of conflict. They awaken empathy where there was indifference. Each Star Child is a node of light in the collective grid of consciousness. Together, they weave an energetic network that uplifts the vibration of the entire planet. The mission of Star Children is not separate from the mission of humanity; it is a mirror. Through their sensitivity, we are reminded to feel. Through their creativity, we are reminded to dream. Through their compassion, we are reminded to love. As their light awakens, so does ours. But we must remember that Star Children are not here to save us; they are here to remind us of what we have forgotten. They call us to remember that we too are made of stardust and soul. Each human, regardless of origin, has the potential to live with this same luminosity. And when humanity finally recognizes that truth, that the Divine lives within all.

Though every Star Child is unique, their missions often fall into a few archetypal roles. These are not rigid categories, but guiding patterns of purpose.

☞ **The Healers**

They bring comfort to pain—not always through medicine or therapy, but through presence. Their voices, touch, or even silent company carry a soothing vibration.

☞ **The Teachers**

Often wise beyond their years, they share new perspectives, not through authority, but through quiet knowing. They challenge outdated ideas and awaken curiosity in others.

☞ **The Creators**

Artists, musicians, inventors, and dreamers—they translate divine frequencies into color, sound, and form. Through creativity, they make spirit tangible.

☞ **The Guardians**

They protect the vulnerable—animals, the planet, or those without a voice. They remind us that love is responsibility.

☞ **The Bridges**

They connect spiritual and scientific, old and new, human and cosmic. They bring integration where others see division.

Every Star Child carries at least one of these roles, though many embody several over their lifetime.

The Inner Mission

Beyond the outer work of helping others, each Star Child carries an inner mission to heal themselves. Before they can lift the vibration of the world, they must reconcile their own duality: their longing for the stars with their life on Earth. Many Star Children grow up feeling different, misunderstood, or alienated. They often carry a quiet homesickness for the stars, a longing for unity and peace that Earth's fragmented world rarely mirrors. Yet, in that longing lies their greatest strength: the ability to connect the higher realms and the Earth through the power of the heart.

This journey of self-acceptance is not easy. Many Star Children feel isolated or burdened by emotions too big for their bodies. Yet every challenge is a sacred initiation, a test of grounding light into matter. When a Star Child learns to love their sensitivity and find a balance between Earth and higher realms, their light multiplies. It no longer flickers under the wind of emotion but shines steadily, guiding others home.

The Role of Star Children Within the Family

Star Children are not above others; they are reminders of what all humans are becoming. They do not come to separate or to stand apart, but to illuminate the dormant light within all beings. Their presence gently stirs remembrance to the human heart that says, "You are divine. You carry the stars."

Their sensitivity and clarity are not signs of exception but reflections of evolution. Through them, we witness what humanity is capable of when heart and soul awaken together. They are connected to natural qualities such as empathy, intuition, and truth, which are the birthright of every soul. Like tuning forks of consciousness, they awaken resonance wherever they go. Their very presence invites authenticity. Their laughter dissolves pretense. Their tears expose truth. Even their silence carries a vibration that reminds others of who they truly are.

Star Children act as frequency anchors, grounding light into dense spaces, balancing chaotic energies, and stabilizing love wherever it is needed most. This often happens without any conscious effort; they naturally recalibrate and harmonize the environments they enter by simply being themselves. A room softens. A heart opens. A conflict begins to unwind. Within families, they are sacred alchemists. Their sensitivity brings to the surface what has long been hidden: the unspoken emotions, unhealed wounds, and love that waits to be expressed. They do not expose these patterns to create pain but to invite healing. Their light reveals where love has been forgotten, allowing it to return. They teach through energy, not instruction. Through them, parents remember how to feel deeply. Siblings learn compassion. Grandparents rediscover wonder. Their presence weaves harmony through generations, mending what words alone cannot touch. These children carry no hierarchy, only frequency. They are not here to lead from above but to awaken from within. Each one is a living reminder that enlightenment is not a privilege, but potential seeded in every human soul. The light they carry belongs to all. When we look into their eyes and see the reflection of the cosmos, we are not witnessing something separate from ourselves; we are remembering our shared origin. And in that remembrance, something sacred awakens: the knowing that the evolution they represent is already unfolding within us.

The new children arriving on Earth are deeply sensitive, intuitive souls who reflect the planet's shifting energy. They come with higher consciousness and awareness of unity, compassion, and truth. Their strong presence encourages families and humanity to evolve. Each generation of Star Children carries a purpose, helping dissolve old patterns and anchor a more heart-centered future. Their sensitivity is not a flaw but a guiding light, inviting us to remember our own inner wisdom and to grow alongside them.

Chapter 3

Signs and Traits of Star Children

Every Star Child carries a unique vibration, yet their essence is woven from similar threads of light. They are sensitive in ways the world doesn't always understand. They are deeply attuned to emotion, energy, and truth. While others see with their eyes, Star Children feel with their entire being. From the outside, they may seem shy, dreamy, restless, or even fragile. But beneath that softness is immense strength: the power of empathy, intuition, and love. These children are like tuning forks, resonating with the energy around them, amplifying harmony when it exists, and trembling when the world is out of tune.

I invite each reader to see their sensitivity not as a weakness but as an evolution for our humanity. Through years of working with many Star Children, I have discovered that while each child is entirely unique, they share common traits.

☞ **Sensitivity to Energy and Emotion**

Before they learn to speak, Star Children are already fluent in the language of energy. They feel before they think. They sense before they understand. When a parent enters the room carrying unspoken tension, they absorb it as their own. When peace fills the space, they breathe more freely. These children read the world not through logic but through vibration. They recognize truth as warmth and falseness as a chill. Their heightened awareness makes them sensitive in ways others may not notice, and even environments with harsh lights, loud noises, rushed energy, or emotional discord can feel deeply overwhelming to them.

Star Children often sense what others feel before a single word is spoken. They may cry without knowing why, withdraw when conflict arises, or comfort others with remarkable intuition. Deeply empathic, they absorb the emotions around them like sponges, which can exhaust them until they learn to release what does not belong to them. Crowds, noise, and chaos can quickly drain their energy, leaving them yearning for calm and stillness.

☞ **Deep Compassion and Connection to All Life**

A Star Child's love is vast and unconditional. They care for animals, plants, and people with the same tenderness. They might cry when they see a tree cut down or an animal hurt. They are natural caretakers and often feel a sacred duty to protect life. This connection comes from remembering unity, the understanding that all beings are expressions of one consciousness.

☞ **Radiant Love and Open Hearts**

Star Children often emanate warmth and unconditional love. Their presence has a calming effect, drawing others toward them as if by invisible magnetism. Even in infancy, they seem to radiate peace. When they smile, it feels like light itself is speaking. Their love is not selective, it flows freely toward people, animals, and even the natural world. Many parents describe feeling healed simply by being near their child's energy.

☞ **A Sense of "Otherness" or Not Belonging**

Many Star Children feel like strangers on Earth. They may say things like, "I don't feel like I belong here," or "I miss home," though they cannot explain what or where "home" is. They may look at the stars and feel a longing that words cannot describe, a deep homesickness for a place beyond memory. This feeling can make childhood confusing, especially when surrounded by a world that values conformity. Yet that very sense of difference is their compass. It reminds them that they came to bring something new, not to fit into what already exists.

- **Strong Intuition and Inner Knowing**

Star Children often "just know" things. They might predict events, sense others' intentions, or offer insights far beyond their age. Their intuition is their natural guidance system, and it connects them directly to higher consciousness. If dismissed or ridiculed, this intuition can retreat inward and cause confusion. But if respected and cultivated, it becomes a lifelong compass of truth.

- **Discomfort with Violence, Dishonesty, or Injustice**

Because Star Children vibrate at a higher frequency of compassion, they struggle in environments filled with anger, cruelty, or deceit. They may cry during the news, refuse to watch violent movies, or question unfair authority. This sensitivity often manifests as anxiety, withdrawal, or rebellion. Yet beneath it lies a powerful moral clarity, and their souls reject what does not resonate with love.

- **Physical Sensitivity**

Many Star Children are sensitive not only to emotions, but also to foods, chemicals, textures, and sounds. They may have allergies, sleep difficulties, or need extra rest. This is not weakness; it is a sign of a finely tuned energetic system. Their bodies are designed to process more light and subtle frequencies, which means they require gentler care.

- **A Natural Draw Toward Spirituality**

Even without being taught, many Star Children speak about angels, guides, or memories of "before I was born." They may recall past lives or describe visions with innocence and certainty. Their spirituality is innate, not learned. They sense that life is more than what meets the eye and often become the quiet philosophers of their families.

- **A Mission-Driven Nature**

Beneath their playfulness and sensitivity lies a serious purpose. Many Star Children speak of wanting to help the world, heal people, or "make Earth a better place." Even at a young age, they may feel pressure to "do something important," which can cause anxiety if they don't yet know how. Their mission is less about what they do and more about who they are. Their very presence raises the vibration of their surroundings.

☞ A Natural Bond with Nature

Star Children are instinctively drawn to animals, plants, and the rhythms of the Earth. They can communicate telepathically with nature and animals. They intuitively understand the healing frequencies of nature and often recharge their energy by being near water, forests, or open skies. This connection reminds us that healing begins through reconnection with the living world.

☞ Creativity and Spiritual Gifts

Star Children are dreamers, visionaries, and artists of the unseen. They express their truth through art, music, storytelling, movement, innovations, and imagination. Many have natural spiritual gifts such as seeing energy fields, remembering past lives, or speaking with spirit guides and angelic beings. Their creativity is not simply a talent; it is a sacred form of communication with higher realms.

☞ Strong Wills and Authentic Spirits

While their hearts are gentle, their spirits are fierce. Star Children possess strong wills, integrity, and a deep desire for authenticity. They are natural leaders who resist control or manipulation. When misunderstood, their strength may appear as defiance, yet at its core lies an unyielding truth; they cannot compromise their inner knowing. Supporting their autonomy while guiding them with love allows their natural leadership to flourish.

☞ Cooperation Over Competition

Unlike traditional models of success that emphasize rivalry, Star Children value collaboration. They thrive in settings that honor equality, shared creativity, and mutual respect. They feel happiest when everyone wins, when connection replaces hierarchy, and when purpose outweighs reward. This cooperative nature hints at the consciousness humanity is collectively moving toward.

☞ **Visionary Thinkers and Innovators**

Star Children often introduce ideas that feel ahead of their time. Their minds are expansive, weaving together logic, intuition, and imagination. Whether designing new systems of education, sustainable living, or technology infused with consciousness, they bring fresh blueprints for humanity's evolution. Listening to their ideas, rather than dismissing them as "fantasy," invites wisdom that may shape our future.

☞ **Multidimensional Awareness and Spiritual Memory**

Many Star Children retain memories of other lifetimes or realities. They may speak naturally about "before I was born" or describe interactions with angels, guides, or celestial beings. These recollections are often vivid and emotionally charged, reflecting an authentic connection to the soul's eternal journey. Instead of dismissing these expressions, parents can gently affirm their experiences, helping the child integrate higher awareness into earthly life.

☞ **A Deep Sense of Unity**

At their core, Star Children feel connected to all of creation. They experience others' joys and sorrows as their own, often showing concern for strangers, animals, and the planet itself. This unity consciousness is both their greatest gift and their greatest challenge. They teach humanity what it means to love without boundaries.

☞ **Emotional Vulnerability and the Need for Nurturing Guidance**

Without grounding and emotional support, their sensitivity can lead to anxiety, sadness, or confusion. Many struggles with feeling "different" or misunderstood. What they need most is understanding, along with gentle guidance that teaches them how to direct their empathy and intuition wisely. With love and validation, their sensitivity transforms into a true superpower.

Star Children are deeply sensitive, intuitive, and connected to energy and emotion. They feel truth instantly, care for all life, and notice what others overlook. Their sensitivity can be overwhelming in a fast or chaotic world, yet it is also their greatest gift. When supported with understanding and calm guidance, they grow into confident, compassionate beings. Above all, these children remind us of a more loving and aware way of living.

Chapter 4

Parents' Inner Healing to Help Star Children Thrive

In a world that often feels chaotic and fragmented, the concept of Star Children offers a hopeful reminder of our potential for spiritual evolution and conscious awakening. We all originate from the stars, carrying within us ancient wisdom and divine purpose. Over countless lifetimes, we have reincarnated into different roles and experiences, sometimes losing touch with our soul's original light. Today, conscious parents are being called to help their children preserve their innate gifts, memories, and spiritual essence. To do so, we must first heal ourselves and create a new, higher blueprint for life on Earth. Our planet stands at the threshold of a profound energetic transformation. Humanity is being invited to release outdated patterns rooted in suffering and fear. The collective trauma passed down through generations, beginning as early as conception, shapes how we experience life, love, and connection. By healing ourselves, we dissolve those old imprints and create space for a higher, more harmonious vibration on Earth.

Unhealed trauma does not simply disappear; it is carried forward through DNA and cellular memory, affecting our children's emotional and physical well-being. This inheritance of pain prevents them from fully expressing their potential. Healing begins by acknowledging our own wounds, bringing compassion to the parts of ourselves that still carry pain.

Trauma can be "big" or "small." Major traumas may include abuse, neglect, violence, addiction, or loss, while subtle traumas often arise from emotional absence, criticism, or conditional love. Both shape a child's worldview and self-perception. When these wounds remain unhealed, they cause emotional disconnection, defensive behaviors, and self-limiting beliefs. The key to transformation lies in awareness. By facing our shadows with love rather than fear, we reclaim the parts of ourselves that were once lost. Healing is not only the transformation of pain; it is the awakening of deeper wisdom. It is a return to wholeness.

When you heal your own story, you free your children from inherited burdens. Whether your child is an infant, adolescent, or adult, your healing has the power to transform your relationship and ripple outward through generations. This is not a journey of blame or guilt but one of growth, forgiveness, and liberation. Every interaction with our child offers an opportunity for healing—both theirs and ours. When we meet conflict with awareness rather than reaction, the energy of generations begins to shift. Dear mothers and fathers, it begins with you. Your commitment to healing and awakening opens the gateway for the Star Children, the luminous souls arriving to help raise the vibration of our planet. Together, we are creating a new reality one heartbeat at a time.

You are not alone on this path. Countless parents are awakening to the same realization—that by healing ourselves, we create a new reality for our children and for humanity. Together, we are writing a new divine blueprint, one that reflects love, awareness, and the boundless potential of the human spirit.

Ancestral Healing: Clearing the Lineage

Each family carries energetic imprints—inherited beliefs, fears, and unresolved emotions passed down through generations. Many Star Children incarnate precisely to help transmute these ancestral patterns. Yet they cannot do it alone. Parents, too, are called to awaken, to bring light into the hidden corners of their lineage. You may notice repeating patterns in your family like, struggles with communication, emotional suppression, perfectionism, scarcity, betrayal, hurt, or shame. These are not coincidences; they are sacred invitations to release what no longer serves.

When you recognize these patterns and choose differently, you alter the frequency of your entire bloodline. But you are the transformer. You are the point of alchemy where pain becomes wisdom and memory becomes light. Healing does not always require revisiting every story or memory. Sometimes, it is as simple as allowing compassion to flow where judgment once lived. It is choosing to forgive those who could not love you in the way you needed, and in that forgiveness, freeing yourself to love your child with greater presence and authenticity.

By feeling what your ancestors could not, you heal what they could not name. Each time you release resentment or soften into empathy, you reopen the river of love that has long sought to flow freely. The moment you declare, "The pain ends here," the current shifts; your child's soul is liberated to live unburdened, creating new patterns of harmony for the awakening Earth. When you choose to heal yourself, you become the bridge between the old world and the new. You end the cycle of pain and begin the cycle of awakening. Your healing ripples through generations, backward and forward, blessing the ancestors who came before you and the descendants who have yet to arrive. In healing yourself, you offer your child a freer future. You show them that growth is not only possible, it is beautiful. You remind them, through your example, that love has always been the strongest inheritance of all.

What Does It Mean—A New Blueprint?

When a new soul enters this world, it carries with it a sacred energetic map, a blueprint formed through countless lifetimes and ancestral experiences. This divine imprint holds the wisdom, lessons, and memories of every generation that came before. Within it lies all that the soul has learned: how to exist in a physical body, perceive through the senses, love, survive, and create.

However, many of these ancestral patterns also contain pain, fear, and limitation, energies shaped by centuries of collective trauma. These lower vibrations often overshadow the higher qualities within the blueprint, guiding life unconsciously through inherited patterns of suffering and separation.

Now, humanity stands at a pivotal moment. It is time to rewrite the blueprint, to deactivate the old codes of pain, scarcity, and fear, and to awaken the frequencies of love, balance, and unity. This transformation begins with each of us. This new divine blueprint is not just a concept; it is a living vibration. Every act of love, moment of forgiveness, and choice to live consciously rewrites the energetic field of humanity. When you release old wounds and embody peace, you shift the frequency of your lineage and set your children free to live from their highest potential.

Reparenting the Inner Child

Before we can guide Star Children, we must walk our own path of inner healing, tending to the physical, emotional, mental, and spiritual wounds that limit our capacity to love fully. This process is not easy, but it is sacred. It means facing our pain with compassion, releasing limiting beliefs, and remembering that healing is not fixing what is broken but embracing what is sacred within us.

Within every adult lives an inner child, the tender, feeling part of us that still longs to be seen, safe, and loved just as we are. No matter how old we are, that part of us always lives in our hearts. Star Children often awaken this part within us. Their laughter, tears, and unfiltered honesty stirs echoes of the times when we were silenced, disciplined, or misunderstood. They call us home to the innocence we once abandoned, inviting us to heal what was left behind. When we tend to our inner child, we reclaim the qualities that make parenting sacred, qualities such as empathy, curiosity, and wonder. We begin to parent not from old wounds but from presence and understanding.

Take moments in quiet reflection or meditation. Imagine your younger self standing before you, perhaps shy, scared, or feeling alone. Ask them what they need and listen with your heart. Then offer them the same unconditional love, patience, and safety that you now offer your own child. When your inner child feels seen and held, your outer parenting softens. You become more intuitive, more patient, and more attuned. The need to control gives way to connection. You begin to see your child not as a reflection of your past, but as a living expression of love unfolding in the present.

Star Children are teachers of this sacred slowing down, embodying authenticity and reminding us to feel deeply and love without conditions. Your healing becomes their foundation. When you soothe your own nervous system, you create an energetic field of safety where they can flourish. When you forgive your own inner child, you free theirs from inheriting your fears.

Each time you offer tenderness to your own wounds, you teach your child how to love themselves. Hold yourself as you wish to be held. Allow laughter and tears to share the same breath. Let joy and sorrow coexist as they always have, for both are gateways to love. You are not broken; you are becoming whole. Through your healing, your child learns that love can hold everything, even the parts once hidden in shadow. When we commit to our own healing, we become radiant anchors of light and compassion for our children. Our transformation becomes the example that helps them shine. And as each of us heals, we contribute to the collective awakening of humanity by paving the way for these luminous souls to thrive.

The Path of Inner Healing

Take a slow breath. Feel the rhythm of your heart, the pulse of earth beneath your feet, and the gentle whisper of the stars above. You are not just a parent; you are a guardian of light, a bridge between worlds, a soul chosen to guide a radiant being into remembrance. As you breathe, let yourself soften. This journey is not about perfection; it is about presence, healing, and returning home to love.

As conscious parents, you hold the sacred responsibility of preparing your bodies, minds, and hearts as vessels of light for the next generation. By healing and elevating your vibration, you create a pure channel through which new souls can enter this world free from the weight of past distortions. Your inner work becomes the foundation for a new human experience—one rooted in compassion, harmony, and awareness. In healing yourself, you give your child permission to remain whole.

Steps to Inner Healing

1. **Self-Reflection:** Take time to examine your life and recognize wounds that still influence your thoughts, behaviors, and your life. Journaling or mindful contemplation can help you uncover patterns that need healing.

2. **Mindfulness and Meditation:** Develop practices that quiet the mind and cultivate inner peace. Meditation enhances self-awareness, helping you stay present and attuned to your emotions.

3. **Emotional Release:** Allow yourself to feel and express emotions through healthy outlets such as art, music, writing, dance, gardening, hiking, physical movement, or anything that speaks to your heart. Emotional expression restores balance and releases stagnant energy.

4. **Seek Support:** Healing is not meant to be done alone. Seek the guidance of a therapist, counselor, or spiritual coach experienced in emotional and energetic healing. Group workshops or conscious parenting communities can also offer encouragement and understanding.

5. **Embrace Self-Love and Compassion:** Practice daily acts of kindness toward yourself. Speak to yourself with gentleness, forgive your past, and honor your growth. When you nurture your own heart, you create an environment where Star Children feel safe to shine.

6. **Grounding Through Self-Care:** Caring for a Star Child requires strong energetic foundations. Their high frequency can sometimes feel overwhelming if you are depleted or ungrounded. Make grounding part of your daily rhythm: walk barefoot, breathe consciously, rest when you need to, nourish your body with wholesome foods, and spend time in stillness. Remember that self-care is not selfish; it is sacred. When your cup is full, your child feels it. Your stability provides them with a sense of safety that words cannot convey.

Here are additional tools to support your healing journey and help you return to balance:

- **Morning Alignment:** Begin each day with a few minutes of quiet breathing. Feel your center before you engage with the world. Spend time to connect deeper to your inner world. Ask yourself, "What I am aware of and grateful for in this moment?"

- **Heart Breathing:** Place your hand on your heart. Breathe golden light into it for three cycles. Whisper silently, "I am safe to love. I am safe to be me. I am love."

- **Mirror Healing:** Look into your eyes in the mirror each morning. Speak words of compassion as if to your own child. For example, "I see you. I honor your path. I love you."

- **Energetic Clearing:** Imagine golden light washing through your body, clearing worry, fear, and inherited energy. Let it expand until your aura feels luminous.

- **Forgiveness Ritual:** Write a letter to your younger self or a parent figure. Pour out everything unsaid, then burn or bury it with intention: "I release this with love."

- **Emotional Awareness:** Each emotion is a messenger. When an emotion arises, ask yourself, "What part of me is this revealing?" Transform reaction into reflection. Listen for the message it carries—the one that invites you to grow and evolve.

- **Energy Hygiene:** Clear your energy daily—visualize golden or white light washing through you or spend time in nature to release heavy densities and emotions.

- **Authenticity:** Speak truthfully. Follow your truth so you don't become energetically depleted.

As you continue this inner healing process, revisit it in a way that feels natural and genuine to you. Use what speaks to your heart and let the rest unfold over time. Make space to care for your inner world. Your emotional state shapes the energetic blueprint of your home and the way your child experiences life. Remember that your outer reality is a reflection of what we hold within. When you nurture your own calm and clarity, you create a steadier, more loving foundation for both you and your child. Each breath of awareness, each act of self-compassion, each step toward your own wholeness is a blessing that extends to your child and beyond. You are not just healing yourself; you are healing your lineage, your home, and the world your child will one day help shape.

Chapter 5

The Star Child as a Mirror

Every Star Child carries a unique vibration, a frequency so pure and crystalline that it illuminates what has long been hidden in the hearts of others. They move through the world with eyes that see beyond illusion and hearts that feel the unspoken truths held by those around them. Their presence alone, gentle yet powerful, acts as a living catalyst for deep awakening and transformation. They do not come to judge, yet their energy often reveals what we have not wanted to see. Some people feel immediate peace and remembrance in their company, sensing a vibration of home. Others may feel unease, resistance, or even confrontation, not because the Star Child has done anything, but because their light reflects what is not healed within us. Their energy is like a mirror of pure light, reflecting not only who we believe ourselves to be but also what we have forgotten, suppressed, or abandoned within. Through them, we meet our own shadows, fears, and longing to return to authenticity.

In this way, Star Children are not merely here to grow, they are here to help us grow. Their souls hold codes of remembrance that awaken dormant aspects of our own divinity. They come to remind humanity of its wholeness to reawaken compassion and restore harmony between heart and mind, Earth, and higher realms.

I would like to share with you some of the great mirrors, the sacred lessons that Star Children bring to support our collective healing journey. These are lessons not of the mind but of the soul; invitations to come home to love, truth, and the radiant unity that has always lived within us.

- **The Mirror of Innocence**

When we gaze into the eyes of a Star Child, we often see something ancient yet innocent, a purity untouched by the heaviness of the world. They remind us of what we once knew before fear and conditioning took root. Their laughter, curiosity, and compassion awaken dormant memories of our own innocence—the time when we trusted the unseen, when wonder was natural and joy effortless. But for some adults, this reflection can be painful. It reminds them of what they've lost or forgotten. In the light of the Star Child's eyes, unhealed parts of the adult soul begin to surface. Rather than interpreting this as conflict, we can understand it as an invitation, a reminder to return to what matters. When a Star Child challenges you, pause before correcting. Ask: "What part of me is being reflected here?"

- **The Mirror of Emotion**

Star Children are natural empaths. They absorb emotional energy like sponges. If there is tension, sadness, or anger in a room, they feel it immediately. They may cry suddenly, withdraw, or act out without knowing why. The emotion they express is not always their own; many times, they are feeling what belongs to someone else. In families, this means that the child's mood can reveal the emotional climate of the home. When they are anxious, perhaps the environment is restless. When they are irritable, perhaps unspoken tension is in the air. Instead of asking, "What's wrong with the child?" ask, "What is the child sensing?" The Star Child mirrors not only individuals but also the collective emotions. They serve as living barometers of harmony and imbalance.

- **The Mirror of Shadow**

The light of a Star Child can also illuminate what others hide like fear, guilt, hate, anger, rage, or patterns of control. Sometimes adults find these children "difficult" because they cannot be manipulated through fear or guilt. They feel falsehood immediately. When a Star Child resists authority, it is rarely rebellion for its own sake; it is an intuitive stand for authenticity. They reveal the shadow in family systems and institutions, where truth is avoided or where love has been replaced by power. Their purpose is not to shame but to bring awareness. If you feel triggered by their intensity or defiance, look deeper. What they reflect may be a truth seeking healing within you, within your family, or in the collective. They are not breaking the system. They are showing where the system was already broken.

- **The Mirror of Love**

Just as they mirror pain, Star Children mirror love with breathtaking clarity. When you show them kindness, they amplify it tenfold. When they are loved without condition, they blossom in ways that inspire everyone around them. They teach through reflection, showing what love looks like when it is given with purity and received with openness. Sometimes their love is overwhelming. Their hugs seem to carry light; their forgiveness is instant. They do not hold grudges. Their love has the power to heal, but only when we let it in. To receive it, we must open the heart and release the armor of self-protection. This is one of their greatest lessons: Love is not earned through perfection; it is remembered through openness.

- **The Mirror of Awakening**

Many Star Children come into families or communities where emotional or spiritual awakening is overdue. Their energy accelerates growth in gentle or dramatic ways. A parent who never believed in spirituality may start questioning life after watching their child sense things unseen. A teacher may soften their rigid methods after realizing how deeply a sensitive student feels.

A family may begin healing old wounds because the child refuses to carry them. Star Children hold a frequency that stirs evolution. Sometimes it shows itself as tenderness, other times as chaos, yet it always carries us toward transformation. Their presence asks everyone around them: "Will you rise to meet the vibration of truth and love that I bring?"

- **The Collective Mirror**

Star Children do not only mirror individuals; they mirror humanity itself. Their compassion reveals the world's lack of empathy. Their sensitivity highlights how numb society has become. Their creativity exposes the limits of conventional thinking. They are showing humanity what must evolve. When institutions fall short in nurturing them, they reveal the systems that no longer nourish the soul, whether it is education that dampens imagination, medicine that overlooks emotion, or leadership that has drifted away from heart. Through them, the world sees its next step: a return to wholeness, balance, and unity. This is why their arrival feels both beautiful and challenging, because they serve as catalysts for change.

- **The Mirror of Light**

Sit quietly for a moment. Imagine standing before a great mirror made of pure light.

In its reflection, you see yourself not as the world defines you, but as a Star Child perceives you. You see the beauty beneath the fear. The strength beneath the pain. The light that has always been there, waiting to be remembered. Now imagine the Star Child standing beside you, smiling. You realize that both of you are reflections of the same divine source, the same starlight shining through different expressions. And in that realization, there is peace. The Star Child is not here to follow us. They are here to remind us of who we truly are.

- **Lessons the Mirror Teaches**

Through their reflections, Star Children teach lessons that words cannot convey.

Lesson 1: Sensitivity is Strength.
They show us that vulnerability is not a weakness but a doorway to empathy, creativity, and genuine connection.

Lesson 2: Truth Heals.
When they refuse to conform to falsehoods, they remind us that integrity is freedom.

Lesson 3: Presence is Power.
They live in the now. They draw us out of mental noise and back into the moment where life actually happens.

Lesson 4: Love Transforms Everything.
Their forgiveness and compassion unveil that love is far more than sentiment; it is a living force that brings transformation.

Lesson 5: We Are All Mirrors.
As we see them reflect us, we realize that we also reflect others, and that healing spreads through awareness.

Healing Through Reflection

When the Star Child's mirror reveals discomfort, we can use that moment as a healing opportunity.

Steps for Healing Reflection:

1. **Pause.** Before reacting, breathe and ground yourself.

2. **Acknowledge the Feeling.** "I feel frustrated/sad/afraid right now."

3. **Ask Within.** "Is this emotion really about the child, or about something I've hidden in myself?"

4. **Accept the Message.** Every emotion is guidance, not punishment.

5. **Transform with Love.** Speak gently to yourself and the child. Let honesty replace control.

When you heal, the child's energy often shifts instantly. Their mirror becomes lighter, and they no longer have to reflect that pain.

✸✸✸

Star Children reflect the emotional and energetic truth of the people and environments around them. Their sensitivity acts like a clear mirror that is revealing harmony where it exists and highlighting imbalance where it needs attention. They reflect innocence, unspoken emotions, hidden wounds, and profound love. Through their presence, they invite parents to grow, heal, and become more authentic. Their reactions are not random; they often mirror the emotional climate of the home or the inner state of an adult. When we feel triggered, challenged, or deeply moved by them, it is an invitation to look within. They reveal both our unhealed parts and our highest potential. In this way, Star Children help families evolve, reminding us that healing, truth, and love always begin within.

Chapter 6

Preparing the Vessel

Conscious pre-conception is a sacred gateway and a time of deep preparation. Preparing for conception is more than a physical act; it is a spiritual initiation. It asks each parent to purify, heal, and elevate so that the child's soul may be welcomed into an atmosphere of reverence and peace. I am inviting both parents to align bodies, minds, and spirits with love, awareness, and intention. When mother and father consciously prepare their vessels to receive a soul, they create the energetic foundation for a peaceful, harmonious beginning. This stage is not simply about preparing the body; it is about aligning the spirit, clearing old patterns so that new life may enter through a field of pure light instead of one shadowed by fear, stress, or unhealed emotion.

Conception, when approached consciously, becomes an act of co-creation with the Divine. Both parents are called to participate equally in this preparation, for conception is not solely biological. It is a sacred journey that creates the doorway through which a new consciousness arrives.

How Parents Can Prepare Their Vessels
Physically–Honoring the Body as Sacred Temple

Your body is the temple through which creation expresses itself. It is both the vessel and the altar of life. Nourish it with intention and gratitude.

- Choose organic, whole, and vibrant foods that carry the Earth's life force.
- Hydrate with pure, living water, and bless it before drinking.

- Replace processed oils such as canola or vegetable oil with natural alternatives like olive, coconut, or avocado oil.
- Rest deeply, move regularly, and honor your body's cycles.
- Release addictions or substances that dull your energy or disconnect you from your natural vitality.
- Treat your body as a living prayer—the sacred ground through which spirit will take form.

When the body is balanced, clean, and alive, it becomes a magnet for higher-frequency souls seeking a peaceful entry into the physical realm.

Emotionally–Clearing the Heart for Love to Flow

The emotional body holds the memories of lifetimes—joy, grief, fear, anger, and longing. To prepare for conscious conception, these emotions must be acknowledged and transformed so the heart can open fully to love.

- Acknowledge any stored pain or unresolved feelings without judgment.
- Practice forgiveness—for yourself, your parents, those who hurt you, and for moments when you forgot your own light.
- Cultivate joy, gratitude, and compassion as your emotional baseline.
- Surround yourself with people and environments that uplift your heart.
- Journal, breathe, and cry when needed. Tears are sacred waters that purify the soul.

When the heart is clear, love flows freely, becoming the frequency through which your child will first experience the world.

Mentally–Aligning Thoughts with Creation

The mind is the architect of reality. Every thought sends ripples into the field of creation. Preparing mentally means choosing thoughts that are in harmony with the life you wish to invite.

- Reprogram the subconscious by transforming limiting beliefs into empowering truths.
- Replace fear-based thinking with affirmations of safety, abundance, and divine timing.
- Visualize yourself as a loving, confident parent, and see your child surrounded by light and joy.
- Read, learn, and expose your mind to uplifting ideas.
- The clearer your mental landscape, the stronger your energetic signal to the universe: I am ready. I am willing. I am love made manifest.

Energetically and Spiritually–Opening the Channel of Light

At the deepest level, conception is an energetic unfolding, a union of soul frequencies guided by divine timing. To prepare spiritually is to purify the channel through which life will flow.

- Practice grounding and breathwork to remain centered and present.
- Cleanse your energy field through meditation, prayer, or time in nature.
- Forgive and release energetic cords that bind you to the past; forgiveness liberates your creative power.
- Invite divine guidance to assist in your preparation—trust that your child's soul is already communicating with you, waiting for the perfect moment to arrive.
- Create sacred space in your home—a quiet corner with a candle, flowers, or symbols of fertility and love—and return to it often in gratitude and prayer.

When your energy is clear, your vibration rises, creating a bridge through which a higher-frequency soul can incarnate with ease and grace.

The Ceremony of Creation

I invite both parents to enter this preparation as a sacred ceremony. Let it be a declaration to the Universe that you are ready to receive life with reverence, harmony, and love. Speak your intention aloud: "We prepare our bodies as temples, our hearts as sanctuaries, and our minds as clear skies through which new life may descend. May this soul feel welcomed, loved, and free."

Conscious pre-conception is not about control; it is about surrender. It is the act of opening fully to the rhythm of creation and trusting that when your hearts are aligned, the right soul will find its way to you. This sacred preparation transforms conception into ceremony, the womb into a temple, and the family into a vessel of awakening. Through your awareness, you are not simply creating life, you are taking part in the rebirth of humanity itself.

Preparing for conception is a sacred and intentional process. It invites both parents to care for their bodies, emotions, thoughts, and energy so they can welcome a soul into a space of peace, clarity, and love. By nourishing the physical body, clearing emotional patterns, choosing supportive thoughts, and grounding spiritually, parents create a strong and harmonious foundation for new life. Conscious pre-conception becomes less about control and more about alignment, a way of saying to the universe, "We are ready to receive with love." When parents prepare with intention, conception becomes a ceremony, and the family becomes the vessel through which a new, higher-vibration soul can enter the world with ease.

Chapter 7

The Journey of Conscious Pregnancy and Birth

Pregnancy is more than a biological process; it is a sacred passage in which two souls, mother and child, weave their destinies together. Within this alchemy, the veil between worlds grows thin. To carry life within is to walk between realms. The mother becomes the bridge through which spirit enters the human form. Her dreams become messages, emotions become language, and intuition becomes compass. In every heartbeat, every breath, and every subtle feeling, she shapes the child's first experience of being human. Her body becomes the first home, her heart the first rhythm, her love the first light the child will ever know.

This sacred union of souls opens a deep remembering in the mother, calling her back to the truth of her divine creative power. She is not simply growing a body; she is calling spirit into form. She becomes both vessel and co-creator, embodying the great mystery of life unfolding through her. When approached consciously, pregnancy becomes a journey of profound transformation. It softens and strengthens her at once, opening her to the vast currents of creation that flow through the cosmos. She begins to feel her interconnectedness with all life—the trees, stars, oceans, and generations of women before her who have also carried the spark of creation in their wombs.

Each phase of pregnancy mirrors the cosmic cycle of birth, death, and rebirth. The mother releases who she once was to make room for who she is becoming, and her emotions, dreams, and body quietly transform in response to this growing love. The child's growth becomes her own evolution. Together, they are not only creating life; they are co-creating higher consciousness.

In this sacred journey, the mother remembers that creation is not an act of effort but a dance with divine intelligence moving through her. When she opens fully to this process, she touches the essence of the universe itself: the eternal rhythm of giving and receiving, of love becoming life.

Conception as Sacred Invitation

Conception is an act of divine orchestration. The soul of the child chooses its moment of entry, drawn by resonance to the frequency of the parents. Some souls hover for years, waiting for the right alignment of love, readiness, and purpose. Others arrive suddenly, like lightning across a still sky, to awaken dormant parts of the heart.

Before conception, the spirit of the child often communicates through dreams, synchronicities, or subtle sensations. A song may move you to tears, a feather may appear, or a sudden warmth may fill your heart, all gentle signals from the soul preparing to join you. When conception is approached consciously, whether through prayer, intention, meditation, or simple awareness, the womb becomes a temple of creation rather than a vessel of chance. The parents' thoughts, emotions, and energy weave the blueprint through which the soul will enter.

Listening Beyond the Mind

Communication with the unborn soul is subtle and multidimensional. It is not always linear, and it rarely comes as clear sentences. Sometimes it arrives as intuition or a sudden knowing that defies logic. Sometimes it is silence filled with presence. Trust that what you feel is enough. The more you release the need to "get it right," the more natural this communion becomes. You do not need special abilities, only openness. Love is the frequency they understand best.

Many parents sense their child's presence before pregnancy even begins. A sudden dream, a vision, or a familiar warmth in the heart may signal that a soul is near. Some feel their child as a soft glow in meditation or as an invisible companion in daily life. This is often the first stage of the soul's invitation, inviting you to prepare emotionally, spiritually, and energetically for their arrival. When this happens, listen. The soul may be communicating what it needs: a more peaceful environment, the healing of an ancestral wound, or a deepening of love between partners. Sometimes it waits patiently until the parents' vibration aligns with its own. Every detail of conception, even timing, unfolds in divine harmony.

The Energetic Field of the Womb

The growing soul rests within this energetic cocoon, absorbing not only nutrients but also frequencies like love, fear, music, silence, and the vibration of words spoken near her body. This is why mindfulness during pregnancy is so essential. Every tender gesture, every soothing word, every moment of gratitude imprints harmony into the developing life. When a woman becomes pregnant, her entire energy body expands. Her aura brightens, her sensitivity heightens, and her intuitive channels open.

The womb is not merely an organ; it is a higher-intelligence field, responsive to energy, emotion, and sound. It holds memory, vibrates with intention, and listens to the whispers of spirit. Many parents do not realize that the womb is a sacred space where a child's physical, emotional, and spiritual foundations are woven into being. Within this nurturing environment, the baby absorbs not only nutrients but also the energy, emotions, and thoughts of the mother. Every vibration, whether loving or fearful, becomes part of the child's earliest imprint on life. When parents first discover they are expecting, their initial emotional response resonates deeply with the developing soul. Joy and gratitude communicate, "You are wanted, you are loved." In contrast, feelings of fear, denial, or anger may leave the baby sensing uncertainty or rejection. This is why it is essential for parents to process their emotions consciously and create an atmosphere of acceptance and peace.

Through many healing sessions, I have witnessed that the emotional experiences of parents during pregnancy profoundly shape a child's inner world. Feelings of love and excitement nurture a sense of belonging, while emotions such as fear, rejection, or shame can create imprints of insecurity and self-doubt. These impressions become the earliest stories written into a child's consciousness. As they grow, these stories influence how they relate to others, how they perceive their own value, and how confidently they move through the world. The womb shapes how a child will perceive the world. It influences emotional stability, physical health, and even spiritual awareness. During pregnancy, the mother's inner world, including her beliefs, relationships, and emotional states, creates the energetic template from which her baby learns about safety, love, and connection. The baby's consciousness is remarkably open and sensitive, absorbing information that will later guide how they respond to life's challenges and joys.

Even before birth, babies are sentient beings. They feel, sense, and remember. As their brains and bodies develop, they are already learning from their environment. They recognize their mother's voice and heartbeat, respond to her emotions, and experience the subtle changes in her energy. Every tender gesture, every soothing word, every moment of gratitude imprints harmony into the developing life. Your baby is aware of everything you feel and experience. As you eat, move, rest, and think, your baby is tuning into your rhythm. The amniotic fluid surrounding the baby even carries the flavor of the foods you consume, allowing your child to begin forming preferences before birth. Choosing nourishing, wholesome foods not only supports physical development but also communicates love and care to your growing child.

Each week in the womb brings new discoveries. Babies spend much of this time in deep, restorative sleep, connected to both the physical and spiritual realms. These quiet moments of floating and dreaming prepare them for their journey to Earth. They are not merely growing, they are also remembering, integrating, and aligning their soul's purpose with the physical body they are preparing to inhabit.

Every soul arrives with great enthusiasm to experience life on Earth, ready to love, learn, and share their unique gifts. When that soul senses thoughts of abortion or adoption, however, it can experience shock, grief, or confusion. Through my work, I've found that such experiences may lead some individuals to later struggle with visibility, fear of rejection, or feelings of unworthiness. Healing these imprints through love and forgiveness allows both parent and child to reclaim a sense of safety and belonging.

Babies communicate with their parents even before birth, often telepathically and energetically. They can feel when you are present, distracted, or emotionally distant. Regularly connecting with your unborn baby helps them feel seen and loved. Speak to your baby softly every day. Whisper words such as, "I love you," "You are safe," "I can't wait to meet you," and "You are always welcome." Your voice becomes a comforting vibration, reassuring them that they are cherished and protected. This daily practice not only strengthens your bond but also nourishes your baby's emotional development. It teaches them trust and establishes a sense of belonging that will guide them for the rest of their lives.

During pregnancy, a baby's awareness is intricately linked to the mother's emotional state. When the mother is calm and centered, her heartbeat beats steadily, and the baby feels safe and peaceful. When she experiences stress or fear, her heartbeat quickens, and her body produces stress hormones that the baby can sense. This creates an energetic message of danger or instability. Conversely, when a mother cultivates serenity and self-care, she transmits vibrations of safety, love, and stability. These become the energetic building blocks of the baby's future emotional resilience.

Through my work with parents worldwide, I've seen a consistent truth: the emotional experiences of the mother and father leave lasting imprints on the child's subconscious. When a mother feels fear, shame, or sadness, the baby often internalizes those emotions as part of its own identity. Because the baby's consciousness exists in oneness, it assumes that everything it senses is about itself. This is why communication, reassurance, and love are vital throughout pregnancy.

Pregnancy often stirs deep emotions such as joy, fear, nostalgia, or even grief. Each feeling is sacred. The conscious mother understands that these emotions are not interruptions to the journey but integral parts of it. Every emotion you feel during pregnancy becomes part of your shared vibration. Joy, gratitude, and peace nourish the child's developing energy field, while fear or stress can create ripples of contradiction. This is not cause for guilt but for awareness. When emotions arise, she does not reject them; she meets them with compassion, saying inwardly, "I see you. I feel you. Thank you for showing me what needs love."

If difficult emotions come forward, there is no need to hide them from your baby. When you meet these emotions with compassion and honesty, you create an energetic field where your child learns that all feelings can be held with love. Your child feels your energy, and what they need most is your calm awareness, not perfection. Place a hand over your belly, take a slow breath, and speak softly: "I love you. You are safe. I am here with you. All is well." If sadness or worry arises, acknowledge it with compassion. "Mommy feels sad today, but I am safe, and I love you." By welcoming every emotion into awareness, she transforms them into light. Her emotional honesty becomes her child's first lesson in authenticity—a knowing that all feelings are safe to feel, and all can be met with love.

I always remind to mothers that the energy of love has infinite power to heal. Simple acts such as placing hands over the belly and whispering, "You are safe. You are loved. We are together," can restore harmony instantly. The unborn child absorbs that vibration and grows in trust. These early experiences become emotional templates, invisible yet lasting. They influence how the child later responds to the world; whether they meet it with fear or curiosity, contradiction or openness.

This conscious communication teaches your baby emotional wisdom even before birth. They begin to understand that emotions are natural, love is constant, and awareness transforms everything. When you honor your own feelings with gentleness, you are showing your child, from their very first heartbeat, that it is safe to feel and love.

Touch is the language of the soul. When you caress your belly, you transmit energy of comfort and connection. Both mother and father should participate in this sacred communication, offering touch, words, and presence. The father's energy of protection complements the mother's nurturing essence, surrounding the baby with balance and harmony. The more you connect consciously with your unborn child, the stronger their sense of belonging becomes. Through your awareness, you are guiding your baby gently from spirit into form, from light into life.

The Mother's Rebirth

Pregnancy is far more than the creation of a child—it is the quiet rebirth of the mother herself. Each moment invites her to surrender more deeply into trust, to move in rhythm with the higher intelligence flowing through her. She stands at a threshold between who she has been and who she is becoming, initiated into a sacred metamorphosis that reshapes her body, spirit, and understanding of love. As the body transforms, so does the soul. Old identities loosen and fall away, making space for new layers of wisdom and tenderness to emerge. Her intuition heightens; her emotional landscape expands. Joy, grief, wonder, and vulnerability rise like sacred tides, moving through her as forces of purification that release what cannot travel with her into the next phase of her becoming.

The soul of the child brings light into every hidden corner. To carry life is to invite awakening. Each emotion, each breath of surrender, each moment of trust becomes part of her own unfolding. She is not only giving life—she is being reshaped by life itself.

When she listens inwardly and allows the process to guide her, she becomes an instrument of divine harmony. Pregnancy ceases to be merely biological and becomes a living apprenticeship in patience, softness, courage, and communion with the creation. She learns that true creation is not an act of control, but an act of surrender to the greater intelligence that moves through all things. Through this initiation, the mother begins to embody the Divine Feminine: receptive yet powerful, soft yet steady, intuitive yet grounded. She does not simply bring a child into the world; she gives birth to an entirely new world within herself, one shaped by deeper love, expanded awareness, and a transformation that touches every part of her being.

As the months unfold, her intuition opens like a flower turning toward the sun. She begins to receive subtle messages such as gentle sensations, inner knowing, and dreams rich with symbolism. The soul she carries communicates through vibration: a flicker of warmth, a pulse of knowing, a soft presence that murmurs, "I am here." And she realizes that communication with her child begins long before birth. Every time a mother places her hand on her belly and breathes with intention, she strengthens the invisible bridge between worlds. Each time she honors her emotions rather than suppressing them, she teaches her child the foundations of emotional safety before the first breath is taken.

It is important to be mindful of the environment around you because it becomes part of the baby's field of awareness. A conscious mother tends to her surroundings by cultivating peace, beauty, and joy. She invites in soft music, natural light, soothing scents, and kind words. Nature becomes her truest ally; the Earth becomes her grounding support. When she walks barefoot on the soil, bathes in sunlight, or breathes the scent of rain, she is nurturing herself. In doing so, she is also teaching her child the vibration of balance and belonging. The more serenity she cultivates within and around her, the more gracefully her baby anchors into the world. In this way, pregnancy becomes both a sanctuary and a shared journey of remembrance, awakening, and profound transformation. In this sacred understanding, she is no longer just giving birth to a child. She is birthing herself anew—as mother, as creator, and as embodiment of the Divine Feminine in motion.

The Power of Stillness

In stillness, the veil between worlds thins. Each pause, each breath becomes a sacred bridge between the seen and unseen. In those quiet moments, when the outer world softens and awareness turns inward, the mother begins to feel the whisper of eternity moving through her. What once felt like silence now reveals itself as the language of the soul. Every gentle inhale becomes an invitation; every exhale is a surrender. Meditation, slow breathing, or simply resting with one hand upon the belly opens the heart to receive what words cannot express. Within this stillness, communication flows effortlessly through vibration. The mother begins to sense her child's presence as light within light, as rhythm within rhythm. She may feel a pulse of warmth, a subtle stirring, or a feeling of being deeply held from within.

It is here she realizes she is not alone. She is surrounded by unseen forces like ancestors who once gave life, angels who guard the threshold, and the consciousness of creation itself moving through her with infinite wisdom. The air around her feels alive, as though the universe is breathing with her. Each still moment becomes a prayer, each heartbeat a message of love between worlds. In this sacred moment of stillness, the boundaries of individuality begin to dissolve. She senses herself as both mother and child. She becomes aware that her pregnancy is a sacred dance of creation between spirit and matter.

Pregnancy teaches that stillness is not emptiness, but the womb of all possibility. In her willingness to rest, listen, or simply be, the mother aligns herself with the great rhythm of life. As she deepens in stillness, fear begins to lose its grip. She no longer approaches birth as something to endure, but as something to remember as a sacred rite of passage encoded in her very being. The same intelligence that formed galaxies is moving through her body. The same breath that flows through all creation now prepares her for the moment of birth. When fear arises, she meets it with breath instead of resistance. Each inhalation gathers courage; each exhalation releases doubt. Her stillness becomes a wellspring of power, which is fluid like the ocean's tide. She begins to trust that her body knows exactly what to do, that her child knows exactly how to come, and that the rhythm between them is already perfect.

This inner peace becomes her strength. She enters labor like one entering a sacred temple, her breath rising as the prayer, her body offering itself as the altar, and her awareness burning as the flame that illuminates the path. The stillness she has cultivated throughout her pregnancy now becomes her compass, guiding her through the intensity of birth with grace and surrender. In the heart of stillness, she realizes that birth is not happening to her but through her. It is the Divine moving in the shape of love expressing itself as life. She surrenders fully to that rhythm, trusting that every wave, every contraction, is a pulse of creation carrying her closer to revelation.

The Energy of Sacred Birth

Birth is one of the most powerful spiritual ceremonies on Earth. It is the moment when the soul fully enters form, and the mother becomes the living doorway between worlds. The energy of birth carries the vibration of creation itself. In conscious birth, fear gives way to trust. The mother remembers that her body is wise, and it knows how to open, how to move, and how to breathe. Each contraction becomes a wave of life-force energy guiding both mother and child toward reunion. When she surrenders to that rhythm, she merges with the creative pulse of the cosmos. Love flowing from partners, midwives, or the Divine weaves an energetic cocoon of protection around the birthing mother. Inside this sacred space, pain eases and her awareness opens, allowing her to feel deeply supported on every level. Many mothers describe moments of timelessness, where the boundaries between self and universe dissolve.

Welcoming the Soul to Earth

The moments following birth are sacred thresholds. It is a pause between worlds where the veil is thin, and the miracle of embodiment unfolds. The baby's first breath mirrors the breath of creation itself. The air entering those tiny lungs is not merely oxygen, but it is consciousness anchoring into matter, spirit remembering form.

How a child is welcomed into the world leaves an imprint deeper than words. Gentle voices, warm skin, soft light, and peaceful surroundings whisper to the newborn: "The world is safe. You belong. I love you." Harsh lights, loud noises, or separation tell a different story. In these first moments, life begins to teach its language through energy, touch, and presence. Hold your baby close, skin to skin and heart to heart. Let your warmth be the bridge between higher realms and Earth. These early moments weave the foundation of trust that will guide their entire life.

Beyond the physical act, birth is an energetic ceremony. Every emotion, every sound, every vibration in the room becomes part of the child's first memory of life. When the atmosphere is calm, loving, and reverent, the soul feels welcomed, and it becomes easier for it to open its light fully. When voices are gentle and touch is kind, when those present remember the sacredness of the moment, the child anchors into the world with grace and ease. This is why it's important for everyone present to remember that they are standing on sacred ground. Each breath, each word, each thought becomes part of the energy the newborn absorbs. The mother's courage, the father's stillness, and the midwife's devotion weave together to create the energetic signature of arrival. This sacred frequency imprints on the child's memory and echoes throughout their lifetime.

The Sacred Dance of Father and Child

During birth, the father's energy becomes a steady pillar and the calm presence that holds the space. His grounding energy creates a sense of safety that allows the mother to let go and focus on the rhythm of her body. His steady breath offers support, like stable earth beneath her waves. His love forms protective field.

In many traditions, the father or partner was not simply watching; he played an active role in welcoming the new soul with respect and care.

When he breathes with the mother, he helps create a shared rhythm that brings calm to the room. Together, they work as a team—supportive, connected, and unified. In this harmony, the child can enter the world gently, arriving not into stress or confusion, but into a space grounded in love.

Birth as Collective Healing

Every conscious birth heals more than one family. It heals the collective story of how humanity enters the world. For centuries, birth was surrounded by fear, control, and separation. Now, a new paradigm is emerging in which birth is honored as a sacred ceremony of light.

When a woman births with awareness, she reclaims her power. When a man stands beside her with reverence, he reclaims his heart. When a child enters the world through love, humanity evolves. Each conscious birth adds light to the collective womb of the Earth, preparing the way for generations of peace. Pregnancy and birth are sacred gateways through which love takes form. When we walk these paths consciously, we welcome not only new life but also a higher frequency anchored in trust, reverence, and light.

Conscious pregnancy and birth are seen as sacred journey where mother, father, and child co-create a new life on both spiritual and physical levels. The mother becomes a bridge between worlds, her emotions, thoughts, and environment shaping the baby's first experience of safety, love, and belonging. Through stillness, conscious communication with the unborn soul, and a reverent approach to birth, the whole family is transformed. Birth becomes not only the arrival of a child, but the rebirth of the parents and a healing offering to the collective.

Chapter 8

The Heart of Conscious Parenting

Conscious parenting does not demand perfection, rituals, or lofty ideals. It asks only for sincerity and the courage to return to the heart. It is not measured by how much we do, but by how deeply we feel and how presently we love. It lives in the small moments like the soft gaze that meets a child's eyes with warmth, the gentle word that steadies an uncertain heart, the shared silence that says, "I am here with you." It is in these quiet exchanges that the sacred reveals itself.

Dear parent, remember this: Your child is not merely a small human being, but a wise and ancient soul who chose you for a reason. There is a sacred contract between your soul and theirs. You were chosen not because you are perfect, but because you are ready to grow. This relationship is not one-directional; it is a circle of mutual evolution, where both souls remember who they truly are through love. Your role is not to mold your child into what you think they should be, but to guide, protect, and nurture them as they unfold into who they already are.

Every soul comes to Earth carrying unique gifts, frequencies, and a purpose that contributes to the whole. When children are seen, honored, and supported in expressing their gifts, they stay connected to their divine essence and grow radiant, confident, and whole. But when fear, control, or unhealed trauma distort the space around them, they can forget their light. They begin to believe that love must be earned, that their truth is too much, or that sensitivity is a weakness. In truth, these moments of disconnection are not failures; they are invitations for us, as parents, to heal the parts of ourselves that long to be seen.

We cannot guide children into authenticity if we are still afraid of our own truth. We cannot model peace if we have not made peace with our own past. Conscious parenting is, therefore, not a method—it is a mirror. It reflects our willingness to return home to love. The conscious parent learns to slow down, listen not only to words but to energy, and see beneath behavior to the need that lies within it. They pause before correcting, breathe before instructing, and meet their child not as an authority, but as a soul in partnership. The child does not need us to be flawless. They need us to be real. Presence is the truest language of love. Presence whispers to the child: "You are safe to be as you are. You are seen. You are felt. You belong."

When we meet a child with openness, grounding, and attunement, something truly miraculous unfolds. Their nervous system settles. Their intuition sharpens. Their sense of self roots in love rather than fear. And in that sacred stillness between hearts, both parent and child remember the same eternal truth: Love is not something we teach. It is who we are.

The Old Blueprint of Parenting

For generations, parenting was shaped by the consciousness of survival. Families did the best they could within systems rooted in fear, hierarchy, and control. Love was often intertwined with expectation, and obedience was mistaken for respect. Parents believed that to prepare a child for the world meant to toughen them, to teach them discipline before tenderness and conformity before authenticity. Many of us grew up in homes where love was conditional, something to be earned through achievement, compliance, or good behavior. Approval was the currency of belonging. Emotions that were too loud, too deep, or too inconvenient were often silenced in the name of strength. Yet beneath this rigidity lay generations of unhealed pain. Our parents did the best they could with what they knew, passing forward the same patterns that once helped keep them safe.

The old paradigm of parenting often expressed itself through behaviors such as:

- Comparing children to others or to siblings, creating competition instead of confidence.
- Setting rigid expectations without honoring each child's unique rhythm or soul design.
- Using material rewards or punishment as substitutes for emotional guidance.
- Dismissing or invalidating emotions with phrases like "Don't cry," or "Be strong."
- Withholding affection when rules were broken, teaching love as something to be earned.
- Exercising authority without empathy, confusing control with leadership.
- Demanding compliance rather than fostering understanding and collaboration.
- Silencing a child's voice or discouraging their natural curiosity and expression.
- Projecting personal frustrations, fears, or unhealed wounds onto the child.
- Manipulating or shaming children into obedience rather than inviting accountability.
- Ignoring emotional needs or exposing them to unstable or unhealthy environments.

These patterns were learned strategies for survival, passed from one generation to the next. Yet their impact runs deep. Such environments teach children to disconnect from their emotional truth, doubt their intuition, and measure their worth through external validation. They learn that to be loved, they must perform. That to be safe, they must shrink. Over time, this conditioning fragments the natural wholeness of the child. They grow into adults who struggle to trust their feelings, speak their truth, or rest in their own being. The lineage of suppression continues, because so few were ever taught another way.

But the energy on the planet is changing, and humanity is beginning to remember the truth. As awareness awakens, so does compassion. We are beginning to see that fear-based parenting does not build strength; it builds walls. I invite you to see the old blueprint, not with judgment toward our parents or ourselves, but with understanding for where our behaviors come from.

Awareness is the first step to true healing. When we look at these inherited patterns with honesty and compassion, we hold the power to transform them. It is time to let go of the old patterns and create room for a new blueprint, one rooted not in control but in connection.

The New Blueprint of Parenting

A new approach to parenting is rising, shaped not by fear or control, but by awareness, empathy, and love. It is a call to evolve beyond the old blueprint of control and conformity and to reimagine parenthood as a path of mutual growth and awakening. Conscious parenting is the art of raising children with presence and emotional intelligence. It begins not with what we do to our children, but with what we cultivate within ourselves. It invites us to pause before reacting, breathe before speaking, and ask, "What part of me is being triggered right now? Am I responding from fear or from love?" This awareness transforms every interaction into an opportunity for healing. Instead of passing forward the pain of the past, we bring consciousness into the present moment. We learn to parent not from inherited patterns, but from truth.

Conscious parenting isn't rooted in perfection but in genuine connection. It's less about behavior management and more about protecting a child's inner being, helping them stay anchored in their light no matter what the world brings. The New Blueprint of parenting calls us to shift from control to connection, authority to awareness, correction to compassion. It is rooted in respecting the child's soul and seeing them not as something to be shaped, but as someone to be understood. It asks us to be guides rather than rulers, to listen rather than dictate, and to model growth rather than perfection. This kind of parenting is a shared soul journey between parent and child. The parent becomes both teacher and student, protector and learner, mirror and companion. Every challenge becomes a doorway to greater understanding; every conflict becomes a mirror revealing where love is being asked to grow.

The new blueprint invites us to embody the following principles in daily life:

- **Love without condition.** Let your child know they are loved—not for what they achieve, but for who they are. Unconditional love builds the foundation of inner security and trust.

- **Lead with empathy.** Listen before you correct. Seek to understand their feelings, even when you cannot agree with their behavior. Empathy opens hearts; punishment closes them.

- **Build emotional safety.** Create spaces where your child can express without fear of judgment or rejection. When feelings are welcomed, emotional intelligence naturally unfolds.

- **Celebrate uniqueness.** Every child carries a distinct frequency—a way of seeing and being that enriches the world. Nurture their individuality rather than shaping them into conformity.

- **Teach inner guidance.** Encourage your child to trust their intuition, to listen to the quiet voice within that knows truth from pretense. This inner compass will guide them more surely than any external rule.

- **Model mindfulness and self-regulation.** Your presence teaches more than words. When you breathe through frustration, you show them peace. When you meet mistakes with grace, you show them courage.

- **Honor sensitivity.** Recognize when your child feels overwhelmed by noise, emotion, or energy. Meet their sensitivity with gentleness, not dismissal. Sensitivity is a sign of depth, not weakness.

- **Encourage creativity and curiosity.** Let exploration be their teacher. Art, music, movement, and nature awaken imagination and help the soul express what words cannot.

- **Communicate with compassion.** Replace threats or bribes with open dialogue. Help your child understand cause and effect through connection rather than coercion.

- **Balance structure with freedom.** Offer routines that ground them, but space that allows discovery. Wholeness thrives in balance between rest and play, solitude and social connection.

- **Model kindness and cooperation.** Children learn how to treat others by watching how we treat them. Every act of respect and patience plants seeds of empathy that will one day blossom in their relationships.

- **Validate their emotions.** Never dismiss their intensity or sensitivity. When you acknowledge their feelings, you teach them that they are worthy of being heard and held.

- **Encourage grounding practices.** Help them anchor their energy through time in nature, mindful breathing, journaling, or quiet reflection. These habits become tools for lifelong balance.

- **Choose environments that nurture the soul.** Education, friendships, and activities should align with the child's essence—supporting not just intellect, but heart, body, and spirit.

- **Practice self-awareness.** Your emotional state becomes the emotional climate of your home. Tend to your own healing because your peace teaches more than your words ever could.

When parents live by this blueprint, the home becomes a sanctuary and a place of belonging. Within such an environment, children grow with open hearts, clear intuition, and a deep sense of self-worth. They learn that love does not vanish when they make mistakes. They learn that their emotions are sacred messengers, not burdens to be hidden. They learn that their voice matters because it is true. This is the new generation of parenting, shaped not by perfection but by presence, and led not by authority but by love. When we parent consciously, we do more than raise children—we raise consciousness itself.

Energy Exchange Between Parent and Child

Parent and child share a sacred loop of energy. When you hold your child, your heart fields synchronize. Science calls it "coherence;" the soul calls it love. The rhythm of your breath, the steadiness of your heartbeat, the tone of your voice all become signals that regulate your child's nervous system. This is why Star Children need physical and energetic closeness. They do not only seek affection; they seek attunement. Being held, rocked, or spoken to softly rebalances their energy. Even older children are deeply moved by this kind of presence, expressed through soft eye contact, gentle touch, or a quiet embrace.

Parents can consciously use this energetic loop for healing. Before touching your child, take a deep breath. Imagine exhaling golden light from your heart into theirs. See any tension dissolving. You don't need words—your energy is the language they understand best.

Conscious parenting is about presence, not perfection. It invites parents to see their child as a wise soul and to lead with empathy instead of control. This chapter highlights the shift from old parenting patterns shaped by fear, comparison, and emotional suppression to a new blueprint grounded in connection, understanding, and emotional safety. Parents learn to slow down, listen, and respond from love rather than old wounds. By modeling calm, compassion, and authenticity, they help children stay connected to their true selves. Conscious parenting becomes a shared path of growth where both parent and child heal, learn, and evolve together.

Chapter 9

The Sacred Journey of Parenting

Parenting is more than raising a child; it is a shared journey of awakening for both parent and child. Through your child, life invites you to rediscover patience, compassion, humility, and unconditional love. It is a mirror unlike any other, reflecting your greatest strengths and deepest wounds. The path of conscious parenting is a continuous dance of learning, healing, and transformation. When we choose to parent consciously, we make a profound commitment: to be fully present physically, emotionally, mentally, and spiritually through every stage of our child's life. It is a vow to listen deeply, respond rather than react, and grow alongside the soul we have been entrusted to guide.

Conscious parenting begins with awareness. The better we understand our children's rhythms, sensitivities, and developmental stages, the more naturally we can support them. When we bring awareness, challenges become bridges to connection, and conflict becomes a reminder to love more wisely. The first seven years of life are especially sacred, as they are a period of energetic imprinting where the foundation of a child's consciousness is formed. During this period, a child's brain operates largely in the theta state, the frequency linked to deep meditative and trance-like states. In this state, the child lives between worlds: open, impressionable, and deeply connected to subtle energy. They absorb not only what we say, but who we are. Every tone of voice, every gesture, every emotional vibration becomes part of their inner landscape. They do not learn through instruction alone, but through the energy we carry, the way we move, and the silence between our words. I invite you to pause and ask, "Am I bringing calm or chaos? Love or fear? Presence or distraction?"

When a child grows in an environment of calm, kindness, and respect, their energy field develops harmony and coherence. Their nervous system learns that the world is safe, love is dependable, and connection is natural. In this soil, trust and creativity flourish. But when a child is surrounded by tension, inconsistency, or unhealed emotional energy, those frequencies are absorbed. They may begin to internalize fear, insecurity, or self-doubt because of what was felt. The child's body remembers what the mind cannot yet name. This is shared not to make you feel guilty, but to help you become more aware.

Perfection is never the goal—presence is. Every moment of reconnection, every apology, every act of tenderness realigns the field. The nervous system, like the soul, is designed to heal. When parents choose to meet their own emotions with compassion, they model the most powerful lesson a child can learn: that energy can always be rebalanced and love can always restore harmony. A deep breath, a gentle touch, a sincere apology—these are not small acts; they are energetic recalibrations that teach repair, resilience, and trust. Your willingness to return, again and again, to love is what builds their foundation of safety in the world. Through your eyes, they learn how to see themselves. Through your touch, they learn how to feel. Through your presence, they remember what it means to be home.

The Power of Example

Your children learn far more from your behavior than from your words. They observe how you speak, respond to stress, treat others, and treat yourself. Each choice you make imprints upon their consciousness, shaping how they relate to life.

If you handle challenges with patience and integrity, they will, too. If you meet mistakes with compassion, they will learn to forgive themselves. Your daily actions become living lessons in love, resilience, and authenticity. Being a parent is one of the most profound spiritual callings and a sacred opportunity to pass wisdom forward through your example.

The Early Years: Birth to Age Two

The first two years of life are among the most sacred. It is a time when the soul begins to anchor fully into the body, and the foundations of trust, safety, and self-worth are laid. During these early years, the world is experienced entirely through the energy of the parents or caregivers. The infant has not yet developed a separate sense of self; they perceive reality as an extension of their emotional environment. Your heartbeat, tone, and presence become their first language.

For a baby, love is felt through warmth, rhythm, and attention. When they are held gently, spoken to softly, and met with consistency, their nervous system begins to organize around safety. They learn that the world is kind, that needs will be met, and that connection brings comfort rather than fear.

Infants are extraordinarily intuitive. They do not yet understand words, but they understand energy perfectly. They can feel the difference between a distracted touch and a mindful embrace, between an anxious voice and a calm one. When a parent is present, relaxed, and emotionally open, the baby's body mirrors that peace. Their breath slows, their muscles soften, and their eyes shine with quiet trust.

When a parent is regularly tense, preoccupied, or emotionally unavailable, the baby feels a subtle imbalance. Because their consciousness is still merging with the world, they interpret this disharmony as something personal. They think, "Something must be wrong with me." This unconscious conclusion can seed early patterns of insecurity or self-doubt that echo into later life.

This is why your presence is the greatest nourishment your baby could ever receive. You do not need to do everything perfectly; you simply need to be there, heart open, eyes soft, attention attuned. When you smile, your baby learns that joy is safe. When you soothe them gently, they learn that emotions can be held, not feared. When you speak with warmth, even without words they understand. "I am loved. I belong." These early experiences form the emotional architecture of your child's inner world. Every affectionate gaze, gentle tone, and moment of comfort sends a message that becomes encoded in their nervous system: "The world is safe. I am seen. My needs matter." This inner knowing becomes the foundation upon which all future relationships are built.

When a child experiences attuned, loving care, they learn deep within themselves that connection is natural and love is dependable. They grow into adults who move through the world with confidence and openness, able to form healthy bonds and express their emotions with ease. The early years are not about stimulation or achievement; they are about attunement. The baby does not need perfection; they need presence. Each time you pause, breathe, and truly see your child, you are building their invisible foundation of safety—one that will carry them for a lifetime.

Ages Two to Seven: The Age of Self-Discovery

Between ages two and seven, children step into a profoundly formative chapter of their soul's path, marked by the blossoming of emotion, imagination, and independence. During these years, their inner world blossoms. They begin to explore who they are, what they feel, and how their actions ripple through the world around them. Their imagination stretches wide, their curiosity deepens, and their emotional range expands to include the full spectrum of human experience: joy and sorrow, delight and frustration, wonder and fear, affection and anger.

Emotions are not obstacles to correct but languages to be learned. Each feeling, whether light or heavy, carries sacred information about their needs, desires, and boundaries. Joy says, I feel connected. Anger says, Something feels unfair. Sadness whispers, I need comfort. Fear asks, Am I safe? Every emotion holds wisdom when met with compassion rather than control.

As parents and caregivers, our role is not to suppress or correct these emotions but to guide children in understanding and expressing them safely. When we honor their feelings as valid, we teach them that they are safe to fully be themselves. When we rush to silence their tears, we unintentionally teach that love is conditional and only certain emotions are welcome. Children who are allowed to feel freely become emotionally balanced and resilient. They learn to move through emotion rather than getting trapped within it. They discover that feelings are temporary—waves that rise, crest, and dissolve—not storms that must be feared.

However, when emotions are labeled as "bad," "too much," or "unacceptable," a child begins to hide parts of themselves in exchange for approval. Over time, this self-protection can lead to emotional disconnection, anxiety, or the habit of people-pleasing. They learn to smile when tears want to rise and comply when their hearts long to speak; through this, they become disconnected from their authentic voice. Creating an emotionally safe environment means giving permission for all feelings, while teaching that actions still carry responsibility. You can say, "It's okay to feel angry, but it's not okay to hurt others," or "It's okay to cry—I'm here with you." These simple words tell the child: Your emotions are valid, and you are not alone inside them.

Remember, children learn emotional regulation not through lectures but through resonance. They watch how you respond when life feels overwhelming. When you breathe through stress instead of reacting, you show them calm. When you speak gently in the midst of frustration, you show them strength. When you apologize after losing patience, you show them humility and repair. Through your example, they learn that love can hold even the hardest feelings.

If your child expresses anger, withdrawal, or sadness, see these not as misbehaviors but as signals of unmet needs. Perhaps they long for attention, affection, or reassurance. Perhaps they need rest, touch, or simply your presence. When you respond with curiosity instead of correction, you teach them that their emotions matter and that safety can be found in relationship, not in suppression. And if you realize there have been times when you were distracted, distant, or reactive—forgive yourself. Parenting is a practice of returning to love, again and again. Every moment of awareness is an opportunity to begin anew. Repair is one of the most powerful lessons a parent can offer. When you apologize, listen without defensiveness, or reach out after disconnection, you teach your child that relationships can heal. Each act of reconnection rewires the nervous system by replacing fear with trust, shame with understanding, and distance with closeness.

Through presence, patience, and compassion, you give your child the greatest gift of all: the freedom to feel and the confidence to know that no emotion will separate them from your love. In this way, the years between two and seven become a sacred classroom—where both parent and child learn the art of emotional truth, love becomes the language that teaches balance, and every feeling, when met with tenderness, becomes a bridge back to the heart.

The Age of Awakening: Seven to Fourteen

Around the age of seven, a subtle but profound shift begins. The child's consciousness, once immersed in imagination and emotional resonance, starts to awaken to individuality. They begin to recognize themselves as separate beings, no longer completely blended with their parents, and they grow more aware of their own thoughts, feelings, and desires. This is the bridge between the innocence of early childhood and the self-awareness of adolescence.

Where the first seven years are devoted to trust and emotional safety, the next seven are devoted to identity and integrity. The child begins to ask questions that reach beyond the surface: "Who am I? Why am I here? What is right? What is fair?" They explore boundaries not to defy, but to figure out what feels honest and authentic for them. During this time, their moral compass begins to take form. They develop empathy, discernment, and a growing sense of justice and compassion. They begin to understand that actions have consequences, words can heal or hurt, energy has impact, and every choice carries meaning. This is the age when the soul's deeper blueprint begins to reveal itself.

As parents, our sacred task is to honor this awakening without extinguishing it. We are called to guide without imposing, listen without judgment, and lead with humility rather than control. The goal is not to shape the child into who we believe they should become, but to create a safe and loving container where their authentic self can unfold naturally.

Children at this age are profound observers of truth. They pick up on everything: your tone, your emotional energy, and the alignment between your words and your behavior. They respond not to authority, but to authenticity. They thrive in environments where they are seen, heard, and trusted to think for themselves. When met with openness, they begin to express their inner world and their dreams. Parents can nurture this stage through meaningful dialogue. Ask them what they think, how they feel, and what they believe. Share your own stories. When you speak honestly, you model that wisdom is not about being flawless but being present, curious, and real.

This is also a time of emotional complexity. The child may swing between confidence and doubt, belonging and solitude, joy and confusion. Their inner landscape mirrors the tides of their transformation. In these shifting seasons, stability becomes your greatest gift. Keep routines simple and consistent. Maintain warmth and boundaries. Let your home be a sanctuary where honesty is safe, mistakes are met with understanding, and growth is celebrated over perfection.

Spiritual curiosity often blossoms during this period. Many children begin to ask profound questions about higher powers, death, energy, and the universe. Rather than providing rigid answers, invite exploration. Encourage wonder. Ask them what they feel or sense. Allow spirituality to remain alive rather than a concept. In doing so, you teach them that truth is not dictated but discovered.

Between the ages of seven and fourteen, sensitivity often deepens before it stabilizes. Some children turn inward, needing solitude to process their expanding awareness. Others grow expressive and bold, testing the strength of their voice. Both expressions are sacred. Your task is to meet them where they are by offering guidance that does not intrude, wisdom that does not overpower, and freedom that does not drift into neglect.

At this stage, children are also absorbing values from the wider world—from peers, teachers, and media. These influences can challenge the principles of home, sometimes creating inner conflict. Rather than responding with fear, anchor your relationship in open conversation. Build a foundation of trust so your child feels safe bringing anything to you, including their questions, their mistakes, and their fears. When a child feels safe to share their truth, you have already created the bridge that will support them throughout the challenges of adolescence. That bridge becomes a sacred connection, reminding them that no matter what they face, there is a steady presence ready to receive them with love.

As they begin to navigate the broader world, they may encounter conflict, comparison, or moments of fear. While we often encourage them to "be strong," it's essential to remember that resilience develops gradually. Before a child can stand firmly in the world, they must first feel safe within themselves. And you are their emotional anchor, their calm in the storm. Teach courage not through pressure, but through presence. Show them what steady strength looks like. Help them process experiences through conversation, validation, and loving reassurance. Let them feel that it's safe to fall apart, safe to express, and safe to begin again.

As they mature, your voice becomes their inner compass—the quiet reminder that says, "I am safe. I am loved. I can handle this." Support them by creating peaceful spaces, teaching grounding practices, and validating their feelings. Encourage creativity, daydreaming, and intuition. Let them know that sensitivity is not a weakness but a gift. Through your mindfulness and balance, they will learn how to stay connected to their inner light, even as the world grows louder around them. The most powerful teaching you can offer is the example of your own truth. Let your actions reflect integrity. Let your compassion be visible. Let your humility reveal that growth never ends. Children learn what love is not through words but through the way we live, forgive, and return to presence.

I invite parents to guide their children gently, hold them with trust, and honor their curiosity as they move through this phase of soul exploration and learning. And as you walk beside them, remember: They are not moving away from you, but toward who they came here to be.

The Adolescent: Fourteen to Twenty-One

Adolescence is a sacred threshold, a bridge between the innocence of childhood and the self-realization of adulthood. It is a time of both expansion and confusion, of inner storms and radiant clarity. During these years, the young soul begins to claim its autonomy, testing boundaries not to rebel against love but to understand freedom.

The journey from fourteen to twenty-one is not merely physical maturation; it is the soul's initiation into individuality. The child who once looked outward for guidance now begins to look inward for truth. They start to question the beliefs inherited from parents, culture, and society. The adolescent's task is to discover who they are beyond expectation, beyond belonging, and beyond the stories that shaped them. For parents and mentors, this stage can feel like standing at the edge of a river watching the one you love begin to cross. You cannot wade the waters for them. You can only hold the lantern on the shore, shining light so they can find their own way.

This is the age when the soul demands authenticity. Teenagers sense when words and energy do not align, when love becomes conditional, or when control masquerades as care. What they need most is not perfection but honesty. They need you to be real. When you admit your mistakes, they learn that humility is strength. When you listen without trying to fix, they feel safe to speak their truth. When you share your own doubts, hopes, and evolution, you show them that adulthood is not the end of growth but the continuation of it.

At this age, emotions intensify. The adolescent's inner world becomes vast, full of passion, confusion, creativity, and longing. Their moods may swing like tides, reflecting the rapid reorganization of their energy and identity. Rather than resisting these changes, meet them with patience and perspective. What looks like rebellion is often a plea for understanding. What sounds like withdrawal is sometimes a search for solitude and self-definition.

Your role is to offer a steady presence, serving as an anchor of calm while their inner world shifts and grows. Continue to offer structure and boundaries, but with flexibility and respect. Replace control with collaboration and punishment with communication. Ask questions that open rather than close: "What do you need right now?" "What do you feel is fair?" "How can we understand each other better?" Such questions invite ownership, accountability, and mutual respect. They transform power struggles into opportunities for connection. Adolescents crave freedom, but they also crave a home base of love that remains constant even as they test the edges of their world. When they know they can return without judgment, they grow brave enough to explore. When they know your love will not withdraw in disapproval, they learn to take responsibility rather than hide in shame.

Spiritually, these years awaken the deeper questions of purpose and belonging. Many young people feel torn between the material world and the call of the soul. They may struggle with anxiety, disillusionment, or the ache of not fitting into conventional molds. Remind them gently that this discomfort is sacred. Encourage them to explore creativity, service, and authentic expression as ways of channeling this energy. Let them know it is okay not to have everything figured out. The soul unfolds in divine timing. Life is not a race to arrive but a journey to remember.

As parents, it is natural to fear letting go. Yet, true love does not cling. To love consciously during this stage means to release control while deepening presence. You become less the teacher and more the witness, less the architect and more the gardener. You water, tend, and protect, but you also allow the plant to reach toward its own light. Celebrate their individuality, even when it challenges your own. Listen to their music, learn their world, meet them where they are rather than where you wish they'd be. Adolescence is not a rejection of the parent; it is the child practicing what it means to become independent. The more you honor their sovereignty now, the more they will return to you later, not out of obligation but out of genuine respect and love.

Between fourteen and twenty-one, young people are building the bridge between idealism and action, dream and discipline, soul and structure. Support them in exploring their passions and values. Encourage them to ask: "What brings me alive?" "What feels true in my heart?" "How can I use my gifts to serve?" These questions awaken purpose. They help the emerging adult align with the essence of who they are meant to become.

By twenty-one, the soul begins to stand fully in its sovereignty. The lessons of childhood and adolescence weave together into a tapestry of self-awareness. If the earlier years were about trust and emotional safety, this stage is about learning to embody authenticity in the world. When parents offer guidance rooted in empathy, the young adult enters life with quiet confidence, equipped with empathy, resilience, and purpose. They know that love is not control, mistakes are teachers, and vulnerability is a doorway to strength.

And for the parent, this stage offers its own initiation—the art of letting go with grace. To watch your child become their own person is both a loss and a liberation. It is the moment when love expands beyond dependence into mutual respect, when your child no longer needs you to survive but still chooses you to share life's journey. This is the sacred gift of conscious parenting: to raise not only a human being but a soul who knows how to love, discern, create, and remember who they truly are.

✹ ✹ ✹

Parenting is a sacred path where both parent and child grow side by side. Our little ones absorb our energy long before they understand our words, especially in the early years when their inner world is shaped by the quality of our presence. It matters how we show up, connect, and listen. When we choose connection over control, calm over reactivity, and honesty over perfection, we create an environment where our children feel safe, seen, and supported. Through each moment of attunement, repair, and love, parenting becomes not just a responsibility, but a shared journey of healing, learning, and remembering who we truly are.

Chapter 10

Creating Sacred Space: The Importance of the Home Environment

The home is more than a physical structure; it is a living field of energy that shapes the emotional and spiritual well-being of every soul within it. It is the first universe your child will know, the energetic womb that continues to nurture and influence them long after birth.

Just as a seed requires fertile soil to grow, children thrive in environments filled with warmth, stability, and harmony. Every thought, word, and emotion exchanged within your home becomes part of its energetic imprint. These vibrations are absorbed by your child and form the foundation of how they perceive the world.

Energy and Emotion in the Home

Star Children are highly sensitive to the emotional climate around them. They intuitively feel the energy of their caregivers and the spaces they inhabit. A peaceful home helps regulate their nervous systems, encouraging emotional balance and a sense of safety. Conversely, homes filled with tension, arguments, or emotional disconnection can create anxiety or insecurity. Even if children cannot articulate what they sense, they internalize it, often mirroring the energy they absorb. This is why cultivating calm, loving communication and emotional presence is one of the most powerful forms of parenting.

The home reflects the inner state of those who dwell within it. When the household feels heavy or disconnected, it is often a call to pause, breathe, and realign. Star Children need authenticity, consistency, and love. When you bring mindfulness to daily routines such as meals, bedtime, or conversations, they naturally become moments of connection. Every hug, every shared laugh, every moment of stillness sends the message: You are safe. You are seen. You belong.

Creating a Conscious Environment

A conscious home is one where love is felt, respect is practiced, and emotions are acknowledged rather than suppressed. Here are simple ways to create such an environment:

- *Infuse the home with intention*: Begin each day by setting a loving intention for your household. Words such as peace, joy, love, and understanding carry powerful vibrations.

- *Clear energy regularly*: Open windows for fresh air, burn sage or incense, use essential oils, or play soothing music. Energy cleansing helps reset the frequency of your space.

- *Create sacred corners*: Dedicate small areas for reflection, meditation, or creativity. These become anchors of peace for you and your child.

- *Model kindness and communication*: The tone between parents becomes the child's internal dialogue. Speak with gentleness—your words plant seeds in your child's heart.

- *Invite nature in*: Plants, crystals, sunlight, and natural materials help children stay grounded and connected to the Earth's nurturing energy.

- *Minimize chaos*: Keep spaces tidy and simple. Clutter holds stagnant energy, while openness allows creativity and peace to flow.

The Art of Energetic Hygiene

Just as we bathe our bodies, we must also clear our energy. Everyday life brings us into contact with many different energies, some uplifting and some draining.

Here are simple practices can keep the family field bright and balanced:

1. Morning Light Clearing
Upon waking, imagine a soft golden light descending from above, filling your body and expanding outward to encompass your home. As it flows, it clears stagnant energy and awakens peace. Invite children to imagine this as well, as it helps them begin their day in a state of clarity.

2. Evening Release
Before sleep, take a few deep breaths and visualize brushing away the energies of the day. You can do this in a literal way by gliding your hands down your arms and torso, as if gently brushing away dust. Invite your children to do it playfully: "Let's shake off the day and keep only the love."

3. Smudging or Sound Clearing
Burning herbs like sage or palo santo, using essential oils, or ringing bells and chimes helps reset the home's vibration. Children often enjoy taking part, walking through each room with a bell or feather in hand. It teaches reverence for energy and gives them a sense of sacred responsibility.

4. Crystals and Natural Elements
Place crystals such as clear quartz, rose quartz, or black tourmaline in the home. Plants, flowers, seashells, or bowls of salt naturally purify energy. These elements remind the family that the Earth supports balance and renewal.

5. Gratitude Invocation
Energy responds to gratitude like sunlight to water. Begin or end the day

with a simple family ritual: "Thank you for this home, for our love, for our peace." Spoken aloud, gratitude infuses the air with harmony.

✶ ✶ ✶

The home is the child's first energetic space where they shape perception about life. The learning happens not through instructions but through feeling and learning the emotions, tone, and intention of those around them. Star Children feel this deeply. A peaceful, loving home helps them regulate, trust, and thrive. When the home is calm, clear, and intentional, children remain grounded in their own light rather than overwhelmed by the disharmonious energies around them. As shared above, the home becomes a true sanctuary when we choose kind communication, keep the energy clear, nurture loving relationships, and spend intentional time in nature. Sacred space is not about perfection; it's about creating an atmosphere where every child feels safe, seen, and held in love.

Chapter 11

The Sacred Role of the Father

Dear fathers,

You are not alone. You are part of a great reawakening of the masculine heart.
Your love is rewriting history.
Your presence is the prayer that builds the new world.

The awakening of the father is the awakening of balance on Earth. As men remember that love is strength and presence is power, a new world begins to take root. In this world, children grow in wholeness, mothers are supported in their sacred role, and families become sanctuaries of light. The rebirth of the father is not a return to power, but it is a return to presence. In this rebirth, the Divine Masculine returns not as a ruler, but as a servant of love with the steady hand that holds, the strong heart that listens, and the grounded soul that protects the light of the new generation. It is the masculine remembering how to bow to the mystery of creation, hold space for life as it unfolds, and honor both the fire and the stillness within. When the Divine Masculine awakens in this way, the family becomes whole.

Star Children are the catalysts of this transformation. They come to awaken not only the mother's lineage, but the father's as well. Their luminous presence calls forth the Divine Masculine to remember its original essence as guardian, not as master, but as protector of life's sacred balance. Through them, men are remembering that to love deeply is not weakness but strength. They are reclaiming their emotional intelligence, intuition, and capacity to feel and nurture. The father's hands, once tools of labor and defense, become vessels of healing. His voice becomes a song of reassurance. His gaze becomes a mirror of safety through which the child knows, "The world is safe because love is here."

From the moment conception occurs, the energetic bond is formed. He may not carry the child within his body, but he carries the vibration of safety around both mother and child. His energy becomes a shield of calm, an anchor that grounds the family in stability. A conscious father does not protect through fear but through awareness. His steadiness provides the container within which the mother can soften, and the child can grow. When his energy is peaceful and focused, the home becomes a sanctuary of trust.

Many men experience a profound transformation during pregnancy and birth. Hearing the baby's heartbeat, feeling a kick beneath the mother's hand, or witnessing the miracle of birth cracks open the heart in ways words cannot describe. This awakening can be both beautiful and disorienting. Old wounds may surface: memories of their own fathers, unmet expectations, or fears of inadequacy. Yet within these moments of vulnerability lies the opportunity for healing. To love a child is to remember the capacity for tenderness that has always lived within.

The father's emotional openness is not weakness; it is divine strength. It teaches the child that masculinity can hold, comfort, and protect without withdrawing or dominating.

Presence Over Perfection

Star Children do not need perfect fathers; they need present ones. Presence is love translated into time, attention, and grounded energy. It is the willingness to pause, listen, and hold space for emotions that may not have words. What children remember most is not the number of hours spent together, but the depth of connection within each moment. When a father kneels to meet his child's eyes, listens without distraction, or shares laughter freely, he is teaching that love is safety, and attention is sacred.

Simple rituals can become powerful anchors: bedtime stories, walks in nature, cooking together, or moments of silence watching the stars. These are not small things; they are threads that weave security and belonging.

The Father as Healer of Lineage

Every father carries within him the imprint of generations. Some carry unspoken grief, others the weight of responsibility, pride, anger, or fear. Yet when a father chooses to parent consciously, he begins to rewrite those ancestral stories. Each time he chooses patience over anger, honesty over avoidance, tenderness over control, he heals the men who came before him. He shows his child that masculinity can be both powerful and kind, strong and soft, protector and poet.

It is crucial for fathers to do their own inner healing so they can become radiant examples of what wholeness looks like in form. In this way, the father's growth extends beyond himself and becomes part of the collective evolution. He becomes a bridge through which the wounded masculine finds redemption. His transformation becomes a light that travels backward through generations, offering peace to those who never had the chance to awaken.

Guiding the Star Child

Star Children arrive remembering the infinite. They sense energies, feel emotions, and often seem to live with one foot in another realm. The father's grounded presence helps them integrate these celestial qualities into human life. He is the anchor that allows their spirit to soar without losing touch with the Earth. His steady love reminds them that this planet, too, is sacred. Through meditation, stillness, or simply mindful attention, fathers can share the gift of spiritual grounding. Sitting together in silence, strolling under the stars, tending the garden, or breathing deeply during stress are simple yet profound acts of spiritual fatherhood. A father's energy and presence teaches Star Children how to bring their visions into the physical world. He is the bridge between higher realms and Earth, helping the child navigate material reality without losing their light. When the father affirms the child's sensitivity and creativity, he strengthens their confidence. When he honors their intuition rather than dismissing it, he helps them trust their inner voice. When he plays and dreams alongside them, he teaches that imagination and action can coexist. The father's encouragement gives the child the wings to soar.

Becoming the Pillar of Peace

To embody the sacred role of fatherhood is to become a pillar of peace. It means showing up each day not as a flawless guardian, but as a conscious being willing to grow. It means listening deeply, speaking truthfully, and holding space with gentleness. When a father lives from this awareness, his presence becomes medicine. His family feels it. The Earth feels it. The child, sensing that stability, blossoms into their own luminous potential.

A sacred father leads not through control but through love that is steady, present, and unwavering. He is the grounding force through which the Divine remembers its shape in form. In moments of conflict or uncertainty, the conscious father leads not by force but by centeredness. He models how to breathe through difficulty, how to return to love even in tension. His child learns emotional regulation not through instruction, but through witnessing peace embodied.

It is time for fathers to awaken to their sacred role. A deep remembering is awakening new codes of masculine strength that is rooted in presence, tenderness, and grounded love. Let go of all fears and old beliefs about what the role of a father should be. Allow your soul to gently guide you through heart-opening healing so you can fully embrace your emotions, softness, love, and joy. It may take time to rediscover the part of you that once felt disconnected, but it has always been there. Give yourself the space to listen and be present with yourself, with your child, with your family, and with nature. Through father-grounded love, he becomes a pillar of peace, a guide for Star Children, and a vital part of restoring balance in the family and the world.

Chapter 12

The Sacred Role of the Mother

Dear mothers,

You are sacred.
Your body is a temple of creation.
Your love is shaping the new Earth.

The mother is the first home of the soul. Before a child opens their eyes to the world, they swim within the ocean of her heartbeat, bathed in her emotions, nourished by her thoughts, and held by her love. Within her body, spirit becomes matter. Within her energy, light learns to take form. Motherhood transforms every aspect of a woman's being: body, mind, heart, and soul. Through conception, pregnancy, birth, and nurturing, the mother becomes a vessel of creation and divine wisdom. In the ancient world, this truth was honored. Mothers were seen as living temples. Today, as the world awakens once again, that sacred recognition is returning.

A Star Child chooses you for a reason because you are ready to walk the sacred path of motherhood in all its layers. As mothers, we become wisdom keepers, protectors of light, creators, and bridges between worlds. Let us walk this path together, remembering our true essence and our inner light. As our consciousness expands, we shift from seeking to define ourselves to stepping into the role of the empowered mother. This mother recognizes her own evolution and allows it to guide how she supports her child. She does not protect them by wrapping them in avoidance but by walking beside them with compassion, presence, and unwavering strength. She is the one who teaches her child how to stay rooted in themselves. She helps them navigate sensitivity instead of suppressing it. She guides them through emotions with awareness rather than fear. Her grounded energy becomes the anchor that allows the Star Child to remain open-hearted in a world that may not yet fully understand them.

The Mother as Creator and Bridge Between Worlds

Mother is the living bridge between spirit and matter. From the very moment of conception, a sacred connection begins between the seen and unseen realms. The mother becomes both vessel and creator, embodying the infinite intelligence of life itself. Every cell of her body awakens to this sacred purpose. Her heartbeat becomes a drum that summons spirit into form. Her breath becomes the wind that carries the soul earthward. Within her, the Divine Feminine remembers her original power as the creative force through which galaxies are born. The mother's intuition heightens as her consciousness expands to include another. She begins to feel life through sensations, visions, and dreams that transcend logic. Her emotions become sacred messengers, translating the silent language of the soul she carries. To be pregnant is not merely to nurture a body, but to weave a soul's destiny into the tapestry of matter. The womb becomes a living altar, a temple of transformation where love takes shape. The woman becomes a cosmic portal, her body rewriting the codes of creation with every heartbeat. To carry life is to remember that you are not separate from creation; you are creation.

The Mother's Energy as the Child's Foundation

A mother's energy forms the foundation upon which her child's world is built. Long before language, structure, or teaching, the child learns through vibration. The mother's emotional well-being becomes the blueprint for how a child experiences safety, connection, and love. In the earliest years, a child does not yet know where they end and the mother begins. Their energies are still intertwined. Her heartbeat, her breath, her calm, and her laughter all shape the architecture of the child's nervous system. When the mother's heart is steady, her frequency becomes an anchor that helps the child settle and expand. When she is anxious, hurried, or emotionally distant, the child may absorb that unease and express it through restlessness, withdrawal, or tears. Star Children mirror energy because they feel deeply. When a mother pauses to center herself before responding, she restores the harmony both she and her child need.

The greatest gift a mother can offer her child is her own peace. Her serenity becomes their sanctuary. Her self-compassion becomes their model for self-love. The more she tends to her inner world, the more her child learns that stability lives within. This is why mothers should be more mindful of their energy and making space for inner healing. Every fear she releases, every moment of self-forgiveness, every breath of peace she cultivates ripples into her child's field, softening patterns of anxiety, scarcity, and separation that families have carried for generations.

As a child grows, they carry within them an echo of their mother's energy. If she remained calm during difficulty, they remember calm. If she met mistakes with compassion, they remember kindness. Her energy becomes their internal compass. A mother's energy is not defined by constant positivity; it is shaped by authenticity. A child feels safest not with a perfect parent but with one who feels, heals, and continues showing up with love. A mother who can say, "I'm having a hard moment, but I'm here," teaches resilience more deeply than one who hides her pain behind a smile.

Star Children feel this even more intensely. Their sensitivity is both a mirror and a guide. When a mother chooses peace, they expand. When she grounds herself, they blossom. When she reconnects with joy, they reflect that brightness in their expressions and laughter. They thrive when their mother's words, actions, and emotions align. Thus, the sacred task of motherhood is not to control every external detail, but to cultivate a vibration of love that naturally radiates outward. This steady field becomes the child's first lesson in living with an open heart in an unpredictable world. To nurture her own energy is to nurture the soul of her child. Her healing becomes their foundation. Her peace becomes their protection.

Her presence becomes their home.

Nothing nourishes a child more profoundly than a mother's presence. Children do not need constant stimulation nor flawless parenting. They crave the quiet reassurance that comes when a parent's attention settles fully on them. Presence becomes the living expression of safety, carried not by words but by awareness and the soft willingness to slow down. When a mother returns to her center, she becomes the still point around which her child's world can move freely. Her peace teaches without speaking; her steadiness becomes the rhythm through which love is remembered.

The Mother as Teacher of Love

From her arms, the child learns the language of love. The rhythm of her heartbeat becomes their first meditation. The tone of her voice becomes their first lesson in trust. Through her, the child learns that love can be both soft and strong. That compassion does not mean weakness. That boundaries are not rejection but sacred self-respect. When a mother honors her child with love and offers that same love to herself, she teaches what true wholeness is. She becomes the living example of balance that her child will carry into every future relationship.

The Mother's Intuitive Wisdom

Every woman holds a deep, ancient intelligence. In motherhood, this intuition blooms fully. A mother often "just knows" when her child is hungry, unwell, or in need of comfort. This is an energetic attunement. For mothers of Star Children, this intuition becomes even more vital. These children communicate not only through words but through energy, dreams, and emotion. They respond to authenticity, not performance. When a mother trusts her intuition, she creates a channel through which divine guidance flows effortlessly, directing her toward what her child truly needs.

✹ ✹ ✹

You have come so far on this sacred journey of conscious parenting and inner transformation. You've discovered new layers of yourself and deepened your understanding of your child. Take a moment now—breathe deeply, place a hand on your heart, and offer yourself the embrace you so often give others. Feel the gratitude of how much you've grown, how much you've healed, and how devoted you've been. Your courage and your heart have brought you here. And if you ever forget, gently remind yourself that it's not perfection that matters, but your presence, healing, and inner peace. These are what become your child's deepest source of stability, safety, and love.

Chapter 13

Guiding and Nurturing Star Children

Growing up, I often felt alone on my soul's journey. My parents, though loving in their own ways, were not able to understand the sensitivities, perceptions, and inner gifts that shaped my world. There was no language for what I felt, no guidance for what I saw, and no one who could help me navigate the unfolding of my deeper awareness. That loneliness became the beginning of my calling.

Over the years, through thousands of healing sessions and my own devoted inner journey, I gathered the wisdom I once needed as a child. I learned how it feels to walk through life with heightened sensitivity and intuitive gifts, and how challenging it can be without understanding or support. This is why I feel so deeply grateful that you are reading these words now. Your presence here tells me something important: You want to truly see your child. You want to understand them, honor them, and walk beside them with awareness. That intention alone already changes everything. There is no single method for supporting intuitive or sensitive children because each one is a universe of their own. I learn this daily with my son. His gifts show up differently than mine ever did, more activated, more expansive, and carrying an even deeper connection to the unseen world. Every day with him teaches me that our children are not here to fit into our understanding, but they are here to expand it. Your child came with a unique blueprint, a distinct sensitivity, and a purpose that unfolds in its own divine rhythm. You are not expected to know everything, however invited to stay open, present, and willing to grow alongside them. And you are already doing that.

I always remind parents that to raise or guide a Star Child is both a blessing and a sacred responsibility. You are not simply nurturing a child; you are tending to a soul of ancient light. These luminous beings enter the world already awake in ways others may not yet perceive. They carry a purity of heart, a quiet wisdom, and a sensitivity so refined that the pace and noise of modern life can easily dim their brilliance. Your role as parent is not to shape them into the world's expectations, but to help them remain true to their own essence. When they are met with love, acceptance, and genuine understanding, their light roots deeply into the Earth, anchoring more fully with each passing day. Your presence becomes nourishment. Your awareness becomes guidance. Your compassion becomes the rich soil in which their consciousness grows strong. Their sensitivity is not a weakness to be managed; it is a sacred instrument. It is a finely tuned compass that allows them to feel truth, sense energy, and navigate life with extraordinary depth. Like any delicate and powerful gift, it requires care, balance, and protection. Every Star Child is a seed of light planted in humanity's soil. Some bloom early, others later. Some change the world quietly, others visibly. Your role is to water them with patience, protect them with love, and trust divine timing. Do not rush their awakening. It unfolds with the rhythm of the stars.

The practices below are offered not as rigid instructions but as gentle pathways to support their subtle energy, honor their intuition, and help them harmonize their inner world with the rhythms of daily life.

- **Create Sacred Rhythms**

Sensitive children thrive in predictability. Gentle morning and evening rituals like lighting a candle, saying a blessing, and sharing a deep breath give them a sense of stability in a world that often feels chaotic. Rhythm is the heartbeat of safety.

- **Honor Silence and Solitude**

Star Children restore themselves in quiet moments. Respect their need for retreat without labeling it as withdrawal. Silence is not emptiness; it is where they return to balance. Encourage gentle alone time for reflection, daydreaming, or reading. During sacred pause, they reconnect to their inner world.

- **Encourage Expression**

Art, music, dance, movement, and storytelling allow emotions to move freely when words cannot. Creativity is their soul's natural language. Provide outlets that help them translate feelings into form like painting, writing, singing, or simply playing in imaginative flow.

- **Model Emotional Regulation**

These children learn less from instruction and more from your vibration. When you breathe through frustration, they learn calm. When you meet pain with compassion, they learn courage. Your emotional integrity teaches far more than any lesson spoken aloud.

- **Ground Through Nature**

Bare feet on the earth. Sunlight on the face. The scent of rain or the hum of bees. Nature restores what screens and noise take away. Encourage daily time outdoors like gardening, climbing trees, collecting stones, or lying in the grass. The Earth reminds them where they belong.

- **Protect Their Energetic Space**

Star Children feel everything. Gentle boundaries, simple routines, and mindful media exposure help preserve their sensitivity as a strength, not a burden.

Holding Space for Star Children with Love and Coherence

Star Children do not respond to fear-based authority; they respond to authenticity, presence, and love. They feel energy long before they process words. They sense sincerity the way others sense temperature. They know when truth is being spoken and when emotions hide beneath polite gestures. To guide them is not to lead through force but through coherence. When you speak, let your energy soften and settle. When you correct, let compassion shape your tone. When you listen, open your heart fully and without agenda. These children flourish not under rigid rules but within relationship rooted in trust, honesty, and mutual respect. Your presence becomes their compass, far more than any lesson you could ever teach.

Their sensitivity is both their greatest gift and their deepest challenge. In a world that often glorifies detachment and toughness, sensitivity must be protected, nurtured, and celebrated, never "fixed." Children learn emotional intelligence not through instruction but through resonance. They study your nervous system more than your words. When they feel deeply, show them empathy. Encourage emotional expression through words, art, movement, or quiet reflection rather than suppression. When they cry, hold space and do not shame their tears. When they retreat, honor their rhythm. When their emotions swell, remind them that feeling is strength, not weakness.

Teach them that empathy is a superpower and that boundaries are an essential form of self-love. Offer them a simple affirmation to carry within their heart: "I can love without absorbing." Because their sensitivity is profound, their environment becomes a crucial guardian of their well-being. A chaotic, loud, or emotionally charged home can flood their subtle system. But calm, beauty, and harmony help them re-center and return to themselves.

Here are some examples that you can incorporate in your house to create a sanctuary of serenity within the home:

- Keep spaces soft, uncluttered, and breathable with plenty of natural light.
- Play gentle music or use calming scents such as lavender, rose, or sandalwood.
- Minimize exposure to screens, loud noises, or harsh, violent imagery.

- Bring nature indoors—plants, crystals, shells, or fresh flowers infuse the space with harmony.

And remember, sometimes the simplest moments like gazing at the sky, resting beneath a tree, or listening to birdsong or wind are enough to reset their nervous system completely. Nature speaks in the language Star Children understand best: slow, gentle, and true.

Teaching Grounding and Balance

It is essential for Star Children to spend regular, unstructured time in nature. Nature is their original home, their energetic ally, and the place where their sensitive systems can release, restore, and recalibrate. Unlike many children who adapt easily to artificial environments, Star Children absorb the emotional and energetic residue of the spaces they inhabit. Their bodies and auras act like tuning forks, picking up discordant vibrations, electromagnetic overstimulation, and emotional density from people, environments, and even technology. In nature, this accumulated heaviness dissolves effortlessly. The Earth knows how to metabolize what their systems cannot. The wind unwinds tension. The trees absorb static and return stillness. The sun strengthens their vitality. Water washes their field clean. Animals mirror unconditional presence and love. Starlight reminds them where they come from.

Star Children often live between worlds—one foot in the subtle realms of intuition, dreams, and higher consciousness, and the other in the tangible world of form. This dual awareness can make them feel unanchored, overstimulated, or "too open" at times. Grounding is the bridge that helps them hold their light in a human body without being overwhelmed by the density of Earthly experience. Grounding is more than touching the soil, but it is an energetic and physiological process. Neuroscience shows that nature regulates the nervous system, guiding the brain into calmer, more coherent rhythms. Research indicates that direct contact with natural ground can reduce inflammation and support emotional balance. Many children who carry intuitive or psychic gifts feel "remembered" by nature in ways human society often cannot provide. For Star Children, grounding practices are soul medicine.

Here are simple ways to support grounding:

- Barefoot contact with grass, soil, sand, or stone encourages energetic release.
- Climbing trees or sitting with their back against a trunk connects them to Earth's stabilizing field.
- Gardening helps them feel the rhythm of creation through their hands.
- Collecting stones or nature treasures builds a tactile relationship with the planet.
- Mindful nature walks help them integrate emotions and experiences without needing to talk.
- Sitting near water—rivers, oceans, or even fountains—clears emotional heaviness.
- Star-gazing strengthens the bridge between their cosmic memory and earthly purpose.

When a Star Child roots into nature, their whole being reorganizes. Their intuition sharpens, their emotions soften, and their inner vision clears. They become more embodied, more confident, more present.

Supporting Emotional Health

Star Children experience emotions not only from within themselves but also from the people and environments around them. Their energy fields are highly porous, absorbing the joys, fears, and tensions of others as if these feelings were their own. Without guidance, this sensitivity can lead to overwhelm, confusion, or sudden emotional shifts they don't understand. Supporting their emotional health means teaching them how to differentiate, process, and release what they carry.

Begin by reminding them that their feelings are not flaws; they are signals, teachers, and invitations. Emotions move like waves. Nothing stays forever, and nothing needs to be suppressed. When children learn to witness their emotions rather than fear them, they develop resilience and emotional intelligence that will support them for life. Supporting the emotional health of Star Children is not about preventing big feelings, but it is about guiding them into a relationship with their emotional world. Through gentle practices, consistent compassion, and the freedom to express themselves, they learn that sensitivity is not a burden. It is a superpower that needs to be honored and understood.

Here are gentle daily practices to help Star Children stay balanced and clear:

- **Cleansing Visualization**

Just as we teach children to wash their hands, Star Children must learn to clear their energy. Invite your child to close their eyes and imagine standing beneath a waterfall of golden or white light. Tell them, "This light is washing away everything that isn't yours—all heaviness, all worries—leaving you bright, calm, and clear." Other simple practices, like deep breaths through the heart, brushing off the body with hands, holding grounding stones, or visualization of a cocoon of soft light. Practice helps sensitive children release energy they've absorbed and return to their natural state of openness.

- **Creative Expression**

Provide safe, welcoming outlets where they can move emotions from the inner world into form. Painting, journaling, music, clay, storytelling, or even imaginative play helps them translate energy into something visible and manageable. Creativity brings relief, clarity, and confidence.

- **Movement and Breath**

Star Children often hold energy in their bodies. Gentle movement like yoga, stretching, nature walks, or dancing helps release emotions and restore balance. Teach them simple breathing practices: "Smell the flower... blow out the candle." Breath is one of the most powerful regulators for a sensitive nervous system.

- **Naming the Feeling**

When they feel something intense, guide them to name it: "Is this sadness? Frustration? Anger? What is your body telling you?" Teach them to ask, "Is this feeling mine or someone else's?" This helps them distinguish empathy from absorption and keeps their emotional boundaries intact. Naming emotion gives it shape and makes it less overwhelming. It also helps them distinguish their feelings from what they may have absorbed from others.

- **Emotional Safe Space**

Create an environment where all emotions are welcomed without shame. Let them know: "It's okay to feel. I am right here with you." This reassurance becomes their internal voice as they grow. Star Children feel the emotions of others as if they were their own. They may comfort a sibling before a tear is shed, or sense when you are overwhelmed even if you are smiling.

- **Energetic Boundaries**

Teach them simple imagery such as: "Imagine a bubble of light around you," or "See a soft shield of color protecting your heart." Such tools empower them to remain open-hearted without becoming overwhelmed. Teach them that it is okay to say, "No, thank you." "I need space." "That doesn't feel right to me." Boundaries protect their intuition from being overshadowed by the world's noise.

The Intuitive Gifts of Star Children

It is your responsibility to protect your child and welcome their gifts without ridicule. Say things like, "I believe you." "Tell me more." "What does that feel like?" Validation is sacred. It teaches them that their inner world is real and trustworthy. Their gifts are natural extensions of their inner sensitivity, purity, and connection to the unseen. Your role is not to teach them intuition, but to protect and nurture what is already alive within them. If they share something mystical like a dream, a feeling, or a vision then respond with curiosity instead of fear. Ask, "What do you think it means?" "How did it feel in your body?" "Did it have a message?" This fosters confidence and clarity.

While each child is unique, many Star Children share common intuitive abilities. These gifts often appear in gentle, subtle ways at first, becoming stronger as they feel safe to express them. Star Children arrive with inner gifts that cannot be taught but only remembered. Their gifts are not acquired through education, nor inherited through genetics. They come from the realms they traveled before birth, from the wisdom stored in their soul across lifetimes. These children sense the world through a wider lens. Their perception reaches beyond logic and into the subtle languages of intuition, feeling, and energy. Star Children possess intuitive gifts that reveal themselves early in life. Some notice emotions you have not spoken. Some dream of places they've never been. Some see colors around people, feel energy shifts in a room, or hear the quiet voice of guidance inside their heart. Others simply "know" without knowing how they know. And there are so many gifts to be discovered like telepathy, telekinesis, and so much more. Other parents of Star Children observe that their little ones are deeply "in tune" with the natural world; they speak to animals, sense shifts in the weather, or express sadness when nature is hurt. These are signs of elemental empathy. For many of these children, nature is their first language. They feel at home and safe with animals, plants, water, and sky.

Helping Them Navigate the World

For Star Children, the world can feel loud, fast, and overwhelming. Their hearts are wide open in a culture that frequently rewards armor. Schools may emphasize competition over collaboration, intellect over intuition, and conformity over creativity. Peers may not yet have the emotional language to recognize the quiet brilliance of a sensitive soul. Your role is to be both anchor and advocate, helping them move through the world without losing themselves.

To support them, consider these loving approaches:

- **Advocate for environments that honor the whole child**

Seek educational settings or create them within your home that value imagination, empathy, curiosity, and emotional intelligence. Children flourish in spaces where their inner world is nurtured as much as their outer achievements. Teachers who understand sensitivity can become allies in helping your child feel safe, seen, and inspired.

- **Remind them that belonging is not the same as blending in**

Let your child know, "You belong because you are you." Authenticity attracts true friendships and soul-connections. When they learn that their light doesn't need to shrink to fit in, they grow into confident, compassionate leaders of their own life.

- **Offer simple energy tools for self-regulation**

Teach gentle practices that help them stay grounded in chaotic or confusing environments:

  – Imagining a soft cocoon of light around their body
  – Taking mindful "quiet breaks" during overstimulation
  – Bringing a grounding object (a stone, a crystal, a small token) to school or outings
  – Breathing into the belly to calm the nervous system
  These tools empower them to remain centered without shutting down.

- **Help them alchemize difficult experiences**

There may be moments when they encounter misunderstanding, jealousy, rejection, or cruelty. Sensitive children often internalize these wounds deeply. Sit with them and say, "What happened to you is not who you are." Then guide them to explore what the experience is teaching: resilience, self-worth, discernment, or compassion. Pain does not diminish their light; it strengthens the roots of their wisdom.

- **Show them that love is more powerful than judgment**

Help them see that while not everyone will understand them, their kindness, truth, and presence have the power to transform spaces and hearts. Let them know that judgment is often a sign of another's fear or unhealed pain.

- **Be their sanctuary**

Create a home where they can decompress, feel their feelings, and return to center. When the world feels unsteady, your presence becomes their refuge. When sensitive children are supported, their sensitivity becomes strength. When they are encouraged, their intuition becomes wisdom. When they are believed, their spirit becomes unshakeable. Their resilience blossoms not from hardening, but from learning that their love, truth, and awareness are far stronger than anything they will ever face in the world.

- **Allowing Them to Lead**

Many Star Children carry ancient wisdom. They may question outdated systems, challenge authority, or imagine solutions far ahead of their time. Listen to them. The new world they came to build cannot emerge from the old mindset. Allow them to teach you as much as you teach them.

Creating a Safe Space for Intuitive Expression

Children remain open to inner gifts when they feel emotionally safe. Judgment, ridicule, or disbelief can close that channel quickly. When your child shares something intuitive like, a dream, a feeling, an insight, you should meet it with curiosity. You might say, "That's interesting. Tell me more about what you felt." "What do you think that dream was showing you?" "Let's notice together how that feels in your body." Over time, your child learns that their inner experiences are valid, and it is safe to share them with you. Avoid labeling their intuitive moments as "weird" or "impossible." Instead, affirm their sensitivity while helping them stay grounded.

Star Children are deeply sensitive, intuitive souls who need presence, understanding, and emotional safety more than anything else. They feel energy before words, and their gifts unfold best when they are met with calm, acceptance, and curiosity. Your role as a parent is not to shape them but to support their natural essence. These children thrive in environments that honor their sensitivity, protect their energy, and validate their inner world. Through grounding practices, emotional attunement, and open-hearted communication, you become their anchor in a world that can feel overwhelming. Guiding a Star Child is a sacred responsibility, and they need your love, presence, and the willingness to grow alongside them.

Chapter 14

The New Earth Family: Co-creating a Conscious Future

Every generation gives birth not only to children but to a new world. The families of today are creating the future. Each home holds a seed of change, and each loving act becomes part of our collective awakening. The New Earth is not a distant place we are traveling toward; it is a state of consciousness we are remembering together. It emerges through the choices we make, the energy we embody, and the love we cultivate within our homes. It is being born moment by moment—through you, your family, and every conscious breath of love.

The New Earth is not a utopia beyond reach but a collective awakening within the human heart. It is a civilization rooted in reverence for life, where compassion replaces competition, where education nurtures imagination rather than conformity, and where leadership becomes service rather than control. In this new consciousness, technology serves awareness instead of distraction. Communities grow gardens of food and friendship. Science and spirituality walk hand in hand, honoring both reason and mystery. And at the center of it all stands the family, the first temple of love, the first school of empathy, and the birthplace of the soul's belonging. When families awaken, the planet heals. The love, awareness, and compassion cultivated inside the home radiate outward, transforming communities, relationships, and the Earth itself.

Family as a Microcosm of the World

What unfolds within a family is a microcosm of what unfolds in the world. Every conflict that arises, every moment of forgiveness offered, every act of listening or compassion shared becomes a pulse that travels outward into the greater human field.

When a parent chooses patience instead of frustration, they anchor peace into the fabric of the world. When a child laughs freely, their joy ripples into unseen realms, softening heaviness far beyond the walls of the home. When a family gathers for a simple meal and pauses in gratitude, they generate harmony that quietly nourishes the collective.

A single household, when rooted in awareness, becomes a tuning fork for humanity. Its energy radiates through invisible currents, uplifting neighbors, communities, and even those who may never meet its members. The tone you set inside your home strengthens the vibration of the Earth itself. Love travels through resonance. It needs no words, no platform, no audience. Each conscious breath, each moment of presence, each choice to soften rather than harden amplifies the frequency of awakening. The family becomes a sanctuary not only for its members but for the entire planet.

Parenting as Planetary Service

Conscious parenting is one of the highest forms of planetary service. Each time you choose compassion over reactivity, presence over distraction, understanding over judgment, you are contributing to the evolution of human consciousness. When you hold your child close and whisper, "You are safe," you do more than soothe a tender heart. You soften the collective fear woven into humanity's history. You remind the Earth itself that gentleness still exists. When you forgive—yourself, your child, your lineage—you open a door through which generations past and future may finally rest. Forgiveness is never private; it dissolves ancient patterns and frees the collective field from inherited grief. When you choose peace in your home, even in moments when tension rises or emotions surge, you emanate peace across the planet. The vibration of your calm becomes a beacon in the energetic grid of humanity, influencing hearts you will never meet. Parenting done with awareness becomes a prayer in motion.

The New Earth is not born through institutions, governments, or policies, but it emerges through families who remember how to love with intention. A conscious home becomes a sanctuary where love is practiced like a language, emotions are honored as teachers, and children learn that their presence is worthy and welcome. Such a home radiates outward, influencing communities, schools, and eventually nations. The family is the seed of the future. When the seed is nurtured in love, the entire garden of humanity begins to bloom.

The Heart as the Family's True Center

The human heart generates the most powerful electromagnetic field in the body. When a parent's heart is calm, it radiates coherence throughout the household. Children feel this instantly. Heart-centered living matters more than any parenting method or philosophy. No advice can replace the healing frequency of embodied love. Each time you pause before reacting, breathe instead of shouting, and listen instead of correcting, you cultivate an atmosphere where peace becomes natural. A conscious family does not avoid conflict; it transforms it through compassion.

Here are a few simple daily practices to help you root your home in love and strengthen the connection you share as a family:

- **Morning Blessing:** Place a hand on your heart and one on your child's. Whisper, "May our day be guided by love."

- **Evening Gratitude:** Share one thing each person appreciated about the day.

- **Heart Circle:** Sit together and pass a small stone or crystal. Whoever holds it speaks while the others listen. This cultivates respect and emotional presence.

- **Family Stillness:** A few minutes of shared silence or prayer recalibrates energy and restores harmony.

These simple moments become the invisible threads of trust that children carry into adulthood as memories of peace that live forever in the heart.

Returning to Earth Consciousness

To raise conscious families is also to repair the ancient bond between humanity and the natural world. The New Earth is not some distant horizon; it is the rebirth of our connection with the living planet beneath our feet. Star Children come already attuned to this wisdom. They understand the language of nature intuitively. They hear the songs of wind and water as if recognizing an old friend. They sense the shifting moods of the seasons and feel comfort in the soft hum of the Earth. Many gaze at the stars with a familiarity that suggests they have not forgotten where they come from.

Invite your children into the living world not as observers but as participants. Let them garden with you, placing their hands in the soil and feeling the pulse of life flowing through roots and seeds. Let them plant trees, learning patience, stewardship, and the joy of giving back to future generations. Encourage them to care for animals with kindness, developing empathy that extends far beyond human relationships. Let them walk barefoot on the earth so they can feel her stabilizing, loving presence rise through their bodies. These simple practices awaken the deep understanding that we are woven from the same elements as the planet we inhabit. That the air in our lungs once flowed through ancient forests. That the water we drink has traveled oceans and clouds. That our bones carry the memory of mountains.

Teach your children that nature is the body of life itself. She is the great mother who holds all beings. When children learn to listen to the whisper of leaves, honor the cycles of the moon and the tides, and recognize the intelligence present in every blade of grass, they begin to feel their deeper connection to all of life. Through these experiences, they learn that caring for the planet is also caring for themselves. They begin to see that healing the Earth supports their own well-being, that tending to life around them strengthens the life within them and that their choices truly matter.

When children grow up in partnership with the Earth, they carry a wisdom that guides entire communities toward harmony. They become protectors, creators, and visionaries of the New Earth. And as we walk beside them, we remember what it means to belong.

Building Conscious Communities

We are meant to support one another along the way. Conscious parenting does not blossom in isolation, but it expands through connection, shared wisdom, and hearts rising together. The New Earth is not built by individuals striving separately, but by awareness forming gently, steadily, across the planet. These are the places where parents, teachers, healers, elders, and visionaries gather, not to measure who knows more but to awaken the wisdom we hold in common. They come not to impose beliefs, but to co-create a space where truth can be felt, expressed, and lived. Within such communities, children are not seen as problems to be managed but as souls to be honored. Adults are not expected to be perfect but to be present. Healing becomes a shared journey and wisdom becomes something that passes fluidly between generations—child to parent, parent to child, elder to youth, youth to elder.

Now imagine community gatherings where creativity flows freely: art workshops beneath trees, music rising from open hearts, stories told as medicine for the soul. Imagine learning environments where curiosity is celebrated, intuition is honored, and sensitivity is seen as a gift. Imagine families coming together to celebrate, share their gifts, or community service rooted in gratitude. In these spaces, cooperation replaces competition. Presence replaces performance and authenticity becomes the highest currency. In conscious communities, children feel seen and supported naturally, and our personal growth is witnessed with compassion. It shows us that raising children was never meant to be done alone but held together as a shared act of love. Conscious communities teach us that we are woven into one another's becoming. When families unite in awareness, we rediscover what humanity has long forgotten that the New Earth is built one connection and one shared moment of love at a time.

The Sacred Task of Remembering

The New Earth does not ask us to become someone different or strive toward an external ideal. It invites us to return to the truth of who we have always been beneath fear, conditioning, and forgetfulness. We are love embodied. We are awareness in motion. We are consciousness learning to see itself through the tender mirror of family. Star Children come into our lives to awaken this remembrance. Through their purity, honesty, wonder, and even their challenges, they reflect the parts of ourselves that have longed to be seen. They are living reminders of our divine essence, catalysts inviting us to return to the wholeness that has always lived within us.

You are not required to have all the answers. Conscious parenting is not a destination but a living journey. The path reveals itself step by step, breath by breath. Each moment of sincerity, each pause before reacting, each choice to return to love becomes a thread in the tapestry of awakening. Even your smallest acts of courage echo through the unseen realms. When your home vibrates with laughter, honesty, and compassion, it becomes more than a dwelling—it becomes a beacon. A sanctuary. A small but powerful temple of light whose resonance extends far beyond its walls. Every time you soothe your child's fears, you soothe the collective fear of humanity. Every act of patience strengthens the grid of peace on the Earth. Every moment of genuine joy becomes a blessing offered to all beings.

This is how the New Earth is born—quietly, humbly, through hearts that choose love when it is difficult, presence when it is tempting to turn away, and truth when it would be easier to hide.

The New Earth does not arise from institutions or systems; it grows through families who dare to remember the sacredness of connection. It emerges through conscious relationships, through the way we speak, touch, listen, and forgive. Love is the highest intelligence, and every moment you embody it, you participate in the evolution of humanity. Through every mindful breath, every kind word, every softened reaction, and every choice that honors the soul, you help creation remember its original purpose—to love, evolve, and shine. Together, we are not merely raising Star Children, but we are raising a new consciousness. We are shaping the vibration of the future. We are remembering, finally, who we are.

The New Earth begins in the home. Families are the gateways to a more conscious world, and every act of love within a home becomes a ripple in humanity's awakening. When parents choose presence, compassion, and intentional living, they shift the vibration of the planet. A conscious family becomes a microcosm of the future. Raising children with love, respect, and emotional attunement becomes a form of planetary service. By creating peaceful homes, nurturing our connection with nature, and building supportive communities, families help restore harmony on Earth. The New Earth emerges not through systems, but through awakened hearts choosing love moment by moment.

Conclusion

As you arrive at the end of this sacred journey, take a moment to breathe deeply and honor yourself. You have chosen to live with awareness, parent with intention, and love with an open heart. This single choice radiates far beyond your own life; it ripples through generations, healing the past and illuminating the future. Conscious parenting is not about perfection, it is about being present. It is about coming back, again and again, to love. It is about showing up with humility, patience, and a willingness to grow. Every moment with your child, whether peaceful or stormy, is a mirror reflecting your soul's evolution. Through your child, life invites you to rediscover wonder, forgiveness, and the timeless rhythm of unconditional love.

The path you walk now is both ancient and new. It honors the wisdom of those who came before you while carrying the light of a new era dawning upon the Earth. By healing your own wounds and releasing inherited pain, you create the freedom your children have always deserved, the freedom to live unburdened by the echoes of the past. You become the bridge between worlds: between the old and the new, fear and love, separation and unity, forgetfulness and remembrance.

Parenting with awareness becomes an act of devotion to life, love, and the awakening of humanity as a whole. It calls you to listen not only to your child's voice but also to the whisper of your soul and the heartbeat of Mother Earth. Together, they guide you toward patience, compassion, and truth. Each word of encouragement, gentle touch, and mindful breath plants seeds of peace in your child's heart. These seeds will one day blossom into empathy, confidence, and wisdom. They will continue to transform our world long after you are gone, carrying forward the vibration of your love.

To create a flourishing human family and a thriving planet, we must remember that every act of conscious parenting is an act of global healing. The way we conceive, carry, birth, and nurture our children determines not only their future but the vibration of humanity itself. When we bring life into the world through awareness, love, and intention, we are participating in something far greater than parenting; we are shaping the consciousness of the next generation. Every moment of mindfulness, word spoken with kindness, and choice made from the heart contributes to a more harmonious world. The call to awaken is no longer a distant echo; it is here now. It invites us to embody the wisdom and compassion our children already carry within them. Through them, we are reminded of what we have forgotten: that life is sacred, love is our true nature, and each soul arrives with a divine purpose.

As parents, we are both guides and students. Star Children teach us as much as we teach them. They mirror our unhealed wounds, our strengths, and our capacity to love. Every challenge they bring is an invitation to grow and meet life with greater patience, humility, and grace. When we heal our own pain, we end cycles of trauma that have traveled through generations. We free our children from burdens they were never meant to carry. When we speak with presence instead of anger, choose compassion over control, and lead with understanding rather than fear, we change everything.

Parenting consciously means awakening to the truth that our children are not extensions of our ego, but expressions of the Divine. They come through us, not from us. Our task is not to shape them, but to remember who they are as radiant souls of light, here to help guide humanity into a new age of peace. This sacred work begins with you. Every time you choose awareness over reaction, forgiveness over resentment, and love over fear, you become a living example of the new human blueprint. Your healing becomes your legacy. Your presence becomes your child's foundation. May we all walk this path together united by one vision: a world where every child is born into love, raised in awareness, and celebrated for their uniqueness. Let us nurture not only our children's minds but their spirits.

Let us protect their innocence, honor their gifts, and help them grow into beings who live with integrity, compassion, and joy.

This is how we birth a New Earth through acts of love, presence, and devotion within our homes and hearts. Together, we are creating the new divine blueprint that restores balance, honors creation, and celebrates the sacred connection between parent, child, and Spirit. The future begins now—within you, within your child, and within every conscious choice you make.

And it all begins with love.
And it begins with you.

PART II

Inner Toolkit for Conscious Parents

The Practice of Self-Care and Self-Reflection

Conscious parenting invites you to turn the gaze inward. Self-reflection is not about self-criticism, but it is about self-awareness. It is the willingness to pause, breathe, and ask, *"What part of me is being called to heal right now? What part of me is speaking right now—love, fear, or conditioning?"* When you reflect honestly, you begin to see that your child is not the cause of your emotions but the mirror revealing them. It invites you to transform what no longer supports your path.

This part of the book invites you to deepen your journey of self-discovery. It encourages you to reconnect with the truth of who you are beyond roles, patterns, and expectations. It also encourages you to gently explore your inner world so you can clarify what truly matters to you, what you wish to release, and what vision of life you feel called to create moving forward.

Use the workbook section below as a supportive space where you can be honest with yourself, allowing you to grow, evolve, and step into deeper self-awareness.

Take a deep breath. Feel your heartbeat. This rhythm connects you to your child, the Earth, and all life. You do not need to have all the answers. You only need to keep choosing love. For love is not a destination; it is the path itself. And as you walk this path, your child learns that love is, and will always be, their truest home.

Awakening Self-Awareness

What unhealed parts of me still long to be seen, heard, and held with love?

_____
_____
_____

How do I speak to myself when no one is listening?

_____
_____
_____

What emotions arise most often in my parenting? What do they reveal about my own healing?

_____
_____
_____

Am I willing to grow beyond my past without taking my child's behavior personally?

_____
_____
_____

Healing Ancestral and Childhood Patterns

What patterns from my own upbringing do I see repeating in my parenting?

_____

_____

_____

How did love feel in my childhood—conditional, distant, warm, or free?

_____

_____

_____

What would I have needed to feel safe as a child, and am I offering that to my child now?

_____

_____

_____

When my child triggers me, what memory or wound does it touch?

_____

_____

_____

Am I ready to end cycles of shame, control, or silence and replace them with empathy and connection?

_____

_____

_____

Understanding Your Relationship with Your Child

Do I see my relationship with my child as a sacred soul agreement?

_____

_____

_____

Have I truly taken time to know my child's essence—their rhythm, sensitivity, and unique energy?

_____

_____

_____

Do I project my expectations or fears onto them?

_____

_____

_____

When they express strong emotions, do I meet them with compassion or resistance?

_____

_____

_____

How does my energy affect the peace in my home?

_____

_____

_____

Living Consciously

What practices help me return to inner peace?

_____

_____

_____

How can I embody calm strength even in moments of challenge?

_____

_____

_____

How do I show myself compassion when I make mistakes?

_____

_____

_____

What can I forgive today—in myself, in my child, in my lineage?

_____

_____

_____

Energetic Boundaries for Conscious Parents

Sometimes we forget that our energy quietly shapes how a child sees the world and learns what love feels like. When your energy is grounded, calm, and clear, your child feels safe to unfold in their own light. Star Children and sensitive souls are deeply attuned to the emotional field of those around them. They sense when your heart is heavy, your thoughts are scattered, or your energy is tired—even if you say nothing at all. This is why caring for your own energy is a sacred responsibility. Your well-being becomes the anchor that steadies your child's world.

Protecting your energy is not selfish; it is an act of love. Healthy boundaries do not limit love, they protect its sacred flow. They allow your compassion to flow without depletion and ensure that your giving arises from wholeness, not exhaustion. Boundaries show children that honoring themselves and others is what creates real harmony.

To hold light for your children is to become a living example of balance. Take time to rest. To breathe. To reconnect with what nourishes you. Spend moments in stillness. Feel your body, listen to your heart, and let the noise of the world fall away. Refill your inner cup through nature, creativity, prayer, gardening, or anything that speaks to your heart. Whatever restores your vitality also restores your capacity to love deeply. Remember that your energy extends far beyond words or actions. Your vibration teaches as much as your voice does. When you tend to your own peace, your child learns peace. When you practice forgiveness, your child learns compassion. When you set boundaries with kindness, your child learns self-respect.

Here are some practices that may support you on your journey of keeping your energy centered.

- Visualize yourself surrounded by light before engaging with others.
- After emotional interactions, release energy through deep breathing or washing your hands in running water.
- Set emotional limits with love—it's okay to rest, to say, "not now," or to step away.
- Maintain grounding practices like gardening, movement, dance, yoga, stretching, walking, or silence.
- 90 seconds of slow breathing before you wake your child.
- Tea in silence outdoors or by the window.
- A short walk—no phone.
- One song you listen to with eyes closed.
- A three-sentence journal: *What I felt/What I needed/One thing I can give myself.*

Deepen Your Journey as a Conscious Parent

Let's continue your journey of self-discovery. The workbook space below is an invitation to explore yourself more deeply and to better understand your child. Let your heart, not your mind, lead the pen. There are no right answers, only honesty, curiosity, and compassion. Each question is a mirror, reflecting where you are and what is ready to unfold. Find a quiet space and breathe before you begin. Let your writing be your connection with your deeper self.

Inner Child Healing and Self-Reflection

What patterns from my own childhood do I still carry into my parenting today?

_____

_____

_____

In what ways do I speak to my child the way I wish my parents had spoken to me?

_____

_____

_____

Where do I still react from pain rather than presence?

_____

_____

_____

When I feel triggered, what part of me is asking for love or healing?

_____

_____

_____

What does my inner child need from me right now?

_____

_____

_____

What have I learned about myself through my child's presence in my life?

_____

_____

_____

Deepen Connection with Your Child

Who is my child, beyond their age, behavior, or personality? What essence do I sense in them?

_____

_____

_____

_____

What do I notice that is unique or special about my child?

_____

_____

_____

What naturally draws their attention or sparks their curiosity?

_____

_____

_____

What activities, subjects, or experiences bring them joy or a sense of calm?

_____

_____

_____

Has my child ever shared dreams, visions, or imaginative stories that feel meaningful?

_____

_____

_____

What are my child's natural strengths—emotional, creative, intellectual, or spiritual?

_____

_____

_____

In what ways does my child express empathy, intuition, or sensitivity?

___

___

___

How do they respond to energy, environments, or the emotions of others?

___

___

___

How do I honor and nurture my child's unique gifts and sensitivities each day?

___

___

___

Energy, Words, and Awareness

How do my energy, tone, and words shape the atmosphere of my home?

___

___

___

When my child mirrors my emotions, what truth are they showing me about my own state of being?

_____

_____

_____

How often do I pause to breathe before responding?

_____

_____

_____

How do I care for my own energy so I can show up as calm and grounded for my child?

_____

_____

_____

What daily practice helps me reset—even in the middle of chaos?

_____

_____

_____

Sacred Relationship and Growth

How has becoming a parent transformed my understanding of love?

_____

_____

_____

In what moments do I feel closest to the Divine through my role as a parent?

_____

_____

_____

How can I bring more play, joy, and laughter into our connection?

_____

_____

_____

What legacy of love and awareness do I wish to pass on to my child?

_____

_____

_____

When you finish writing, close your workbook and place your hands over your heart.

Say out loud to yourself, *"I am growing. I am learning. I am healing. Through love, I become the parent my soul came here to be."* Let your words rest in the silence that follows. Every reflection is a seed of transformation planted in the garden of your heart.

The Art of Sacred Self-Care

As I shared earlier, a parent's energy is the silent language a child learns first. Your presence becomes the blueprint your child uses to understand emotional regulation, self-worth, and how to relate to the world. Your nervous system sets the tone for your home. Your calm becomes their calm. Your rest teaches them that stillness is safe. Your boundaries show them that self-respect is love in motion. When you nourish your mind, body, and heart, you strengthen the energy you bring into your home, your relationships, and your child's world. When you forget, remind yourself that caring for yourself is not selfish; it is how you sustain your light so you can guide others with clarity, presence, and love.

I invite you to create unique daily practices that replenish your energy, allowing you to return to love. The following examples are just gentle invitations to feel, soften, and align your vibration with your highest truth. Self-care is the way you honor the sacred within yourself, so you can more fully hold the sacred within your child.

☞ **Morning Alignment**

The way you begin the morning sets the vibration for your entire home. Before the world rushes in, take time to connect inward. Even five minutes of stillness can transform how you move through the day.

1. The First Breath
Before opening your eyes, place one hand on your heart and one on your belly.

Whisper inwardly, *"Thank you for this breath. Thank you for this new beginning. Thank you for this precious gift—life itself."* Feel your breath fill your body with light. Feel gratitude expand in your chest.

2. Morning Grounding

Stand barefoot outdoors, if possible. Visualize roots growing from the soles of your feet deep into the earth. With each exhale, release any tension or anxiety. With each inhale, draw up strength and calm from the soil beneath you.

3. Gentle Movement

Stretch, sway, or move with awareness. Allow your body to awaken slowly. As you move, affirm, *"I am grounded, open, and aligned with peace."*

4. Intention Setting

Before tending to your child or the tasks ahead, pause to set an energetic tone for the day.

You might say aloud, *"Today, I choose patience. I choose to listen more than I react. I choose love as my guide."* Children feel the vibration of your intention long before they understand your words.

☞ Throughout the Day Alignment

Parenting often unfolds in motion—dishes, schedules, emotions, and interruptions. But even within this movement, presence can be your constant companion.

Mini Practices to Recenter:

- **The Pause:** When emotions arise, stop, take three conscious breaths, and feel your feet on the ground. This single pause resets your nervous system.

- **Speak Energy, Not Words:** Before responding, check your tone. Soften your voice. Your child feels your energy more than your instruction.

- **Gratitude:** Each time you notice something beautiful, pause and say, "Thank you."
  A moment of gratitude opens the heart again.

- **Touch with Awareness:** When hugging your child, place one hand on their back and one over your own heart. Feel your heartbeats synchronize. This shared stillness teaches safety beyond words.

- **Nature Moments:** Step outside. Look at the sky. Breathe. Even one minute with the Earth can clear emotional fog and dense energies.

- **Nourish yourself:** With food that feels alive and grounding.

- **Take mindful pauses throughout the day:** Place your hand over your heart and breathe until you feel present again.

- **Create boundaries that honor your energy.** Saying no when you need rest teaches your child that self-respect is sacred.

☞ Evening Integration

Evenings are sacred pauses between the busyness of the day and the rest that restores us. It is time to release the day, forgive what was imperfect, and return to harmony.

1. Release and Reflect

After your child falls asleep, sit quietly and ask:

- Where did I stay present today?
- Where did I lose connection?
- What did I learn about myself and my child?

Journal these reflections with compassion, not judgment. Growth begins in honesty.

2. Energy Cleansing Ritual

Light a candle or simply close your eyes and imagine a golden light washing over you, clearing away the energy of the day. Say out loud, *"I release what is not mine. I return to peace."*

3. Gratitude Prayer

List three moments of love—small or big—that blessed your day. Feel their warmth expand through your chest. This simple act raises your vibration as you drift into rest.

4. Evening Bonding

Before your child sleeps, take a quiet moment together:

Speak a gentle blessing, such as, *"You are loved. You are safe. You are light."*

- Share one thing you each appreciated about the day.
- This practice teaches emotional reflection and strengthens your sacred bond.

☞ **Weekly and Monthly Renewal**

Conscious parenting requires consistent renewal. Your energy, like your child's, needs cycles of stillness and replenishment.

Weekly Self-Care Reset

- Spend a few hours in solitude—no distractions, just you and your breath.
- Reflect on what feels aligned and what feels heavy.
- Release what no longer serves you.
- Do something that restores your joy.

Monthly Reflection

At the end of each month, revisit your journal and ask:

- How has my relationship with myself changed?
- How has my energy influenced my child's behavior?
- What am I learning about love?

Then, write a simple affirmation to guide the month ahead and as a reminder of your evolution.

AFFIRMATION:

| |
| |

Practice: Reclaiming Your Energy as a Parent

Being a parent can be tiring, especially when you spend so much time caring for others that you forget to care for yourself. Often, we lose touch with our inner peace simply because we are exhausted, and yet the responsibilities of parenting and providing continue. It is important to notice the early signs of exhaustion and give yourself the time and care your well-being needs. This practice would help you to realign your energy and return to your center. You may do it at the end of the day, before sleep, or whenever you feel drained or scattered. Let it be your quiet practice of remembrance.

Find a quiet space where you can be undisturbed for at least 10-15 minutes. Sit comfortably, close your eyes, and allow your breath to soften. With every inhale, feel yourself drawing in peace. With every exhale, release what no longer serves you. Notice if your mind is wandering and just keep focusing on your breath. Now bring your awareness to your heart. Imagine a soft, golden light glowing there, expanding gently with each breath. This light is your pure essence. It is the same light your child recognizes and feels safe within. See this light expand, filling your entire body. Your mind is clear, your emotions balanced, and your spirit grounded. Let the light form a gentle field around you, shimmering like morning sunlight. This is your sacred boundary that allows peace to stay and negativity to pass through without harm.

Now, imagine your child or loved ones standing within their own circle of light. See each of you radiant, whole, and connected by love—yet free to be yourselves. Breathe in the beauty of that balance: closeness without entanglement, love without exhaustion, care without control. When you are ready, say out loud, "I hold my light with grace. I give from fullness. I love from peace."

Take a few more deep breaths and allow this warm golden light to fill your whole being. Feel your feet grounded to the Earth and your heart open to the light. Carry this calm into your day. Know that every time you return to your center, you show your child how to find theirs.

Daily Affirmations for the Conscious Parent

As you rise each morning and rest each night, remember that you are gently held on this path, always supported and never alone. Each breath of awareness ripples through generations. Each act of patience becomes a seed of peace. Each moment of love, however small, shapes the vibration of the world your child will inherit. You are the keeper of light within your family. Your presence is your offering. Your love is your legacy. Read these words slowly. They are gentle anchors to return you to your heart whenever the day feels heavy.

Morning Affirmations–To Begin the Day in Presence

My breath grounds me, my heart guides me, and my spirit leads with love.

I am calm, grounded, and centered in love.

I choose to show up with kindness and presence.

I release yesterday and welcome today with trust.

Today, I choose peace, awareness, and gratitude.

I choose patience over reaction and curiosity over control.

I see my child with clear eyes as the soul they truly are.

I trust myself to guide with wisdom, compassion, and grace.

I release the need for perfection. My presence is enough.

I carry peace into my home through my tone, energy, and touch.

I am a channel of light.

I honor my child's spirit as I honor my own.

Love is my teacher.

Take a deep breath. Feel the vibration of those words settle into your body and your heart. Thank you, dear parents, for all that you do.

Evening Affirmations—To Close the Day in Peace

I forgive myself for the moments I was impatient or distracted.

I honor the lessons of today and release what no longer serves.

My child and I are growing, healing, and awakening together.

I trust that love repairs all things.

I am grateful for the laughter, challenges, and grace of this day.

I choose rest without guilt, knowing that renewal is part of love.

My heart is open, my body is safe, and my spirit is at peace.

I bless my child with light and wrap them in the energy of the golden light of protection.

I return all worries to the universe and surrender to peace.

I sleep in harmony and feel held by love.

A Guided Meditation for Conscious Parents
RETURNING TO PRESENCE

Find a quiet place where you can sit or lie down comfortably. Let the light be soft.

If you wish, hold a small object that brings you peace. Close your eyes. Take a slow, deep breath in through your nose. Exhale gently through your mouth. Let the day begin to soften around you.

1. Grounding

Bring awareness to the soles of your feet. Imagine roots extending down into the earth—deep, wide, and glowing with golden light. With each breath, feel yourself becoming heavier, steadier, and more connected to the ground beneath you.

Say silently or aloud, *"I am safe. I am here. I am connected to my soul."*

Let your shoulders drop. Let your jaw relax. Let your entire body relax. Let your breath become the rhythm of stillness itself. Stay here for 5 minutes and let your natural breath gently restore your inner peace.

2. The Breath of Light

Now, imagine breathing in a soft light. It can be any color that feels soothing to you. As you inhale, feel this light enter your body, filling your chest with peace. As you exhale, release all tension, fear, self-judgment, or any other feelings.

Inhale—light.
Exhale—release.

Now, notice where you feel that overwhelming sensation in your body. What message is it trying to share with you?

With each breath, you are clearing the space between thought and love. You are returning to your natural state of calm awareness.

3. Heart Connection

Place one hand on your heart and the other on your belly. Feel the warm energy flowing through your hands. Now, visualize your child surrounded by light. See a golden thread of energy connecting your hearts. It glows softly with love, trust, and peace. Say out loud to your child's soul, *"You are loved. You are safe. You are free to be who you are."*

Breathe in—love from your heart to theirs.
Breathe out—peace from your soul to their soul.

Know that they feel you. Presence transcends distance. Love knows no separation.

4. Returning to the Self

Bring your awareness back to your own body. Feel the breath moving gently through you.
Say out loud, *"I am present. I am whole. I am love in action."*

Allow this energy to ripple through your being. Feel the energy moving from the top of your head to the soles of your feet. Let it wash through your cells and entire being like a waterfall. Feel your energy more aligned. Take one final deep breath in. Exhale with gratitude. Sit for a moment in stillness. Notice any sensations or messages within you. When you open your eyes, carry this calm into your interactions, your home, and your heart. Each time you return to this practice, you strengthen the field of love that surrounds your family.

Gratitude and Light

A message of appreciation and a heartfelt blessing for parents and Star Children everywhere.

This book was written from my heart as a prayer, a guide, and a remembrance of who we truly are. Each word was born from my own journey through healing, motherhood, and awakening. My deepest wish is that it serves as a mirror for your own light, reminding you of the infinite wisdom and love that already live within you.

Thank you for allowing me to walk beside you on this sacred path of conscious creation and parenting. Your willingness to expand, heal, and love more deeply contributes not only to your family's evolution but to the awakening of our entire planet. Every shift you make within yourself uplifts humanity.

To all mothers, fathers, and guardians walking this journey, I honor you. You are the keepers of the new light. You are the bridge between worlds, anchoring the Divine into the human experience. Your courage to parent consciously shapes the next generation of awakened souls.

May this book continue to guide you long after you close its pages. And always remember that you are never alone. We are all co-creating a more harmonious world together.

A Blessing for You and Your Child

Let your heart remain open—
a vessel of compassion, courage, and radiant light.

Find calm within each wave of change,
trusting the unseen currents
that carry you where love intends.

Let your home be a sanctuary
of laughter that heals,
tenderness that restores,
and truth that sets the spirit free.

Let your child grow in the brilliance of their own light—
confident in their gifts,
free in their becoming,
rooted in the knowing that they are whole.

See them walk this Earth
with courage and compassion,
remembering always that they are one with the Source,
woven into the great heart of life.

Allow healing to move through your lineage—
softly, wisely,
clearing the echoes of pain,
blessing all that has been,
and all that is yet to come.

Trust your intuition as sacred guidance.
Honor your emotions as holy messengers.

Celebrate your unfolding
as the divine masterpiece it has always been.

And let love—pure, conscious, eternal—
become the ground beneath your feet,
the breath within your body,
the silence between your thoughts,
the light you carry forward.

With infinite love and deep gratitude,

— **Anastasia Spencer**

Acknowledgments

My deepest gratitude to everyone who has supported, inspired, and believed in this vision.

To the mothers, fathers, and children whose stories and healing journeys have touched my heart—thank you for your courage and trust. You have been my greatest teachers.

To my family and friends, for your patience, love, and encouragement along this path of creation—your presence has been a constant blessing.

To my son, whose light continues to awaken my purpose and deepen my understanding of unconditional love.

And to the Divine Source of all life—thank you for the guidance, wisdom, and grace that made this work possible.

With infinite love and gratitude,
Anastasia Spencer

About Author

Anastasia Spencer is a spiritual teacher, intuitive healer, kids and teens yoga/mindfulness/extra sensory abilities teacher, and conscious parenting guide dedicated to helping families awaken to love, awareness, and emotional freedom. Drawing from years of experience in hypnotherapy, trauma healing, and energy work, she supports parents in transforming generational patterns and creating nurturing environments where both children and parents can thrive.

As the founder of *Our Dream Academy for Gifted Children* and the creator of *The Sacred Birthing and Pregnancy Journey Workbook*, Anastasia blends spiritual wisdom with practical guidance to empower families worldwide. Her mission is to inspire parents to raise the next generation of conscious, compassionate beings—the Star Children who will help shape a more harmonious world.

She lives her message every day through the joy of motherhood, the love of her son, and the belief that every family can become a sanctuary of light.

Visit her online at www.portalofrebirth.com

Continue your journey with more books by Anastasia Spencer:

www.portalofrebirth.com/books

www.ingramcontent.com/pod-product-compliance
Lightning Source LLC
Chambersburg PA
CBHW080414170426
43194CB00015B/2805